5 HABITS OF A WOMAN WHO DOESN'T QUIT

Nicki Koziarz

FOREWORD BY LISA ALLEN

B&H
PUBLISHING GROUP

NASHVILLE, TENNESSEE

978-1-4336-9010-5

Publishing by B&H Publishing Group

Nashville, Tennessee

Dewey Decimal Classification: 248.843

Subject Heading: WOMEN \ CHRISTIAN LIFE \ PERSISTENCE

3 4 5 6 7 8 9 10 • 21 20 19 18 17

For years, I felt like a failure in my faith and in my calling because I quit something every week. Sometimes I turned in my resignation. Other times I secretly quit in my heart. But every time I gave up on ministry, threw in the towel on motherhood or called it quits on God, I wondered what was wrong with me. Why didn't I have the courage to persevere? If only I would have had *5 Habits of a Woman Who Doesn't Quit* by my friend Nicki Koziarz! If you're looking for a friend who gets you and who won't let you give up on yourself or your God, this book is for you! Packed with life-changing perspectives and stick-to-your-bones wisdom, Nicki has written a blueprint we'll turn to again and again, and a resource we will want to give all our friends!

Renee Swope, best-selling and award-winner
author of *A Confident Heart* and Proverbs 31
Ministries radio cohost

Five Habits of a Woman Who Doesn't Quit is bold, funny, transparent and practical. Nicki Koziarz will challenge you to evaluate your patterns, and give you practical handles for change. This book is a gift.

Holly Furtick, pastor's wife, Elevation Church

Only read *5 Habits of a Woman Who Doesn't Quit* if you want to laugh while being encouraged by Nicki's stories and her fresh perspective on the Bible. Guys, 5 Habits is not just for the ladies; we can learn from Nicki's wisdom and her transparency. To know Nicki is to love her and the joy of the Lord that she has comes through in this book. Make this your next group book study, you'll be glad you did.

Alan Patterson, campus pastor, Elevation Church

If you've ever felt like giving up on something, *5 Habits of a Woman Who Doesn't Quit* is the encouragement you need to help you press on. Because of Nicki's refreshing transparency you'll be able to connect your struggles to hers as she leads you to never settle for less than God's best. This is a fantastic resource!

Lysa TerKeurst, *New York Times* best-selling author and president of Proverbs 31 Ministries

I know how to quit things. Nicki does too. This is a fun and inspiring book about not quitting. It's about hanging in there and seeing the beauty in staying when you feel like bolting. Nicki doesn't tell us to just take a longer view of our circumstances, but a more accurate one of ourselves and what God might do if we didn't quit. *Five Habits of a Woman Who Doesn't Quit* won't make you want to be like Nicki; you'll want to be more like Jesus.

Bob Goff, best-selling author and speaker

Do you start out of the chutes with great ambition, but soon lose your steam? Ever vow to tackle projects, but then feel like the projects tackle you instead? If you are a quitter who longs to quit quitting, this book is your God-sent solution. *Five Habits of a Woman Who Doesn't Quit* will empower you to finish up instead of fizzling out, reaching your goals effectively. Highly recommended!

Karen Ehman, *New York Times* best-selling author of *Keep It Shut* and *LET. IT. GO.*, Proverbs 31 Ministries speaker, wife, mother, and recovering quitter

To my Grandma LaFave,
whose dream to write became
fulfilled in the next generation

Contents

Habit One: *She accepts the assignment of refinement.*

Habit Two: *She follows through with her commitments despite how she feels.*

Habit Three: *She stays open to the movement of God.*

Habit Four: *She gives others what she needs.*

Habit Five: *She moves forward in faith.*

Foreword

I'm a woman who works out on a regular basis. But the other day as I drug myself through my typical workout, something in me wanted to give up. I contemplated quitting the last five minutes of my workout when Nicki's words about being a woman that doesn't quit rang in my head, "*A committed woman learns to choose what she wants most over what she wants now.*"

That day, I finished my workout because of what I had just read in *5 Habits of a Woman Who Doesn't Quit*.

As a life coach, speaker, and Executive Director of Ministry Training, I'm more passionate about *transformation* than just a lot of *information*. We can read books filled with great information; but if it doesn't lead us to become different and be transformed because of what we read, then it's just a terrific story.

And that's what *5 Habits of a Woman Who Doesn't Quit* offers—*transformation*.

This book put practical application in my hands combined with biblical truth that will help me achieve my goals and live my best life. Whether you need to persevere through a hard marriage, career goals, or lose that last few pounds, this book will help you uncover the obstacles you're tripping over to cross your finish line.

The five habits that pour forth from Nicki's teaching about Ruth take a familiar Bible story and shake out fresh insights that translate into real action in our lives.

Do you want to keep your word? Reach your goal? Stretch your comfort zone? Chapter after chapter will serve as motivation and wisdom.

Once you jump into these pages, you will find yourself wanting to call a girlfriend, coworker, or family member to share quote after quote that will challenge you and really make you think. Who doesn't love a book that naturally builds our private perseverance, but also creates the desire to share with those closest to us? Personal development and community building all in one resource!

I have watched Nicki struggle with giving up personally and professionally, yet muster up the courage, with God's help, to conquer quitting. Even while writing this book, I know it would have been easier and more convenient for her to just put it off. But Nicki allowed me and others, to encourage her to the finish line. She'll do the same for you in this book, support you to finish!

The book you're holding is because Nicki is a woman who doesn't give up. I'm so grateful she pressed on and you will be too.

—Lisa Allen, Executive Director of Ministry Training at Proverbs 31 Ministries

A Letter to Quitters

To the Quitters,

I get you.

I am you.

I run when things get hard. I quit when I don't like how things are turning out. The thought of staying planted anywhere makes me feel like it's going against the grain of who I am. In fact, this book you're holding almost didn't happen.

Because hello, my name is Nicki, and I've quit everything. *I'm not even exaggerating.*

I quit this process more times than I can count. I quit pursuing it. I quit trying. I quit praying for it. I quit believing God for it.

But the day came when I got fed up with my cycle of defeat. And since then, I have been a woman on a mission to reverse the effects of quitting on my life.

I began by going back. Back to my faith, back to my dreams, back to my hopes, and back to the woman I wanted to become. With the foundation and goals in full view, I had to go back and ask these types of questions:

When did you start to believe you are weak? you are not able? you want to quit? you need to give up? you don't deserve to win?

I realized all the things that were keeping me stuck in the process of failure: my thoughts, my insecurities, my low self-esteem, and my disbelief in myself. I discovered I am in fact my own greatest enemy. And one day I had enough. I said, "No more."

By myself I survived defeat temporarily. But the cycle would sneak back up on me. I felt like I was made to eventually quit. I needed someone I could get behind and learn how to break the cycle of defeat, failure, and quitting.

I found her. Her name is Ruth. And friend, this woman had more determination, commitment, drive, and belief than any woman I've ever actually met. Her story is found in the Bible. And Ruth taught me five life-changing habits.

Habits that have helped me find bravery in the midst of this quitting battle. These five habits have messed with me in the best possible ways. They help me stay when I want to run. I definitely don't have these habits perfected, but they have kept me in process.

And through this internal reflection of mine, I've discovered I'm not alone. There are others who are just sick and tired of feeling like a loser. So one day I took these private thoughts and had a public conversation with others about defeat. Instead of judgmental glares, I found the words "me too" to be the connector of our souls.

I don't want to quit, but I do. *Me too.*
I feel like I don't have what it takes. *Me too.*
I want to run away. *Me too.*
I can't stick out most commitments I've made. *Me too.*
I've yet to meet someone who hasn't quit something in her life. You and I need this process. We are bent but not completely broken. There's too much at stake to settle.
I promise I'm way more messed up than you. I've quit more than you've ever quit. I almost missed it. It was almost too late for me. But it wasn't. Change has stayed possible.
Will you strive to be a woman who doesn't quit?
Your dream is not dead. Hope is still a possibility. It's not over.

With you and for you,

Nicki Koziarz

1

Assignment Accepted

Habit One: She accepts the assignment of refinement.

Has anyone ever told you they couldn't count on you?

It's definitely not the most awesome sentiment to receive. Especially when it seems to come out of nowhere! Which is exactly how this entire journey began for me.

He leaned against our painted white cabinets with his arms folded across his chest and shook his head in annoyance. Was he joking? I couldn't even believe the shocking words he just spit out of his mouth. It was about to turn into a word war zone in the Koziarz house.

With a trip to Africa just a few weeks away, Kris, my husband, came home from work that Friday night mumbling something about me needing to bake cookies and wash cars the next morning to help raise funds for his trip.

But I had a *few issues* with his mumbling.

First, I was like, *Kris, really?* Car washes and bake sales are for junior high students. Second, I did not remember agreeing to participate in such a *fun* festivity. I even checked our family calendar app to make sure I hadn't forgotten a prior agreement between us, but this was **not** on the schedule.

And third, I had already planned out my whole Saturday. I simply could not understand why he was unable to see everything I had going on and why participating in this fund-raiser was not my top priority.

Someone has to drive these three girls of ours through six car lines a day, get the nail polish out of the carpet, wash three hundred loads of laundry, chase the dog down the street from the angry UPS man, work part-time, and cook meals no one likes. I do not have the energy for car washes and bake sales. Especially ones I didn't remember agreeing to help with!

The silence through dinner was deafening, and all I could think about were those rude words he spoke to me.

I was too someone he could count on!

Did our kids always get picked up from school? Yes. Well, there was that one time . . . and then that other time.

And oh yes, the time I thought the other carpool mom was picking up? #whoops

Did he have dinner to eat that night? Yes.

Did he have clean socks on? Yes. And I know they weren't matching, but they were clean!

Undone from this trying day, I laid my tired head on the pillow. My final thoughts of the day concluded I was as dependable as they came! And if he couldn't see that, it was his issue, not mine.

All was well in my safe, selfish world until about 5:30 the next morning.

It's pretty unlawful to wake up at 5:30 on a Saturday morning without an alarm clock, but there I was. Wide awake. And angry. Kris's words from the night before hovered over my thoughts. He made clear he felt I was a commitment dropout. I totally disagreed, but why were his words bothering me so much?

I tried to go back to sleep. But I knew the coffeepot would be my only companion for this early hour emotional confrontation. So I made my way downstairs and poured myself a hot cup of self-pity.

On the white couch, with the coffee and the muddy-puppy-paw-print stains, is where I began to have an unexpected encounter with God. My Bible sat on the cushion next to me. So I opened it up and started to find a verse to help me sort through all this emotional exhaustion I was feeling about the situation.

Honestly, I was looking for a verse to help justify my feelings. Tell me you've done this too? But I opened to this verse that was just rubbing me *all wrong*.

"Whoever is faithful in very little is also faithful in much." (Luke 16:10)

My eyes wandered over those words for about ten minutes. And, for the first time in my life, I wondered if I was someone who could be trusted with much.

Personal Agendas

As I wrote in my journal that morning, my soul began to ache. I arrived before God with a personal agenda.

Bless me, O God, in my selfishness, in my disobedience, and in my pride.

Taking our personal agenda to God and asking Him to bless it is always dangerous and detrimental. I felt this deep sense of conviction. Since my husband told me he couldn't count on me, I wondered if God feels that way too?

> Taking our agenda to God and asking Him to bless it is dangerous and detrimental.

I began to recall many things I had agreed to do in my heart but never followed through in my actions. Commitments like turning to God

4

instead of food. Being slow to become angry. Loving others more than myself. Giving generously and doing what I said I would do.

This situation with Kris wasn't the first time I had to confront my commitment issues. I'd been promising more than I delivered for a lifetime. I had been a quitter and a runner from all things.

But adversity brings the opportunity to introduce us to ourselves in a new way. And the way I had approached my lack of commitment before was just to live in a state of denial. This time something felt different inside me.

The whole situation was so internally conflicting because I'm a woman who has a longing to be used by God. I want my life to count for something more than just fulfilling my own desires. I have dreams to make a difference in my generation for the good.

As I sat there reflecting on Luke 16:10, my spirit could sense God's disapproval with my decision about not going to the fund-raiser. All I could think about was this verse, my dreams, and how closely connected everything was. It was as if God were whispering:

If you can't be trusted with *this*, how can you be trusted with *that*?

Intentional steps of obedience mean more to God than we might realize. We want God to do great things in and through our lives, but many of us find ourselves wading through daily discouragement. Sometimes discouragement is brought on by our own decisions of disobedience.

I've discovered lately that this season has been more about God being able to trust and count on me through each and every commitment I make. In God's eyes the "big" things I want to do for Him mean just as much as the "little" things I'm called to do daily.

> Sometimes discouragement is brought on by our own decisions of disobedience.

That early, quiet Saturday morning, I was challenged to see my life for what it really was. But also, to do something about the places that needed to be changed. And I knew I was in the wrong.

So I went upstairs and told my husband I was sorry and I would love to go to the fund-raiser. Okay, I didn't really say I would *love* to go, but, you know, I said I would be there. And I could tell Kris appreciated my gesture.

But something deeper happened in my heart that day. I let God show me something about myself that was an area of weakness: following through with my commitments. My selfish ways were exposed, and this area of my life went through a rebuilding process. It's been one of the most uncomfortable and challenging places to ever walk through.

But while it wasn't easy, that day I began to experience the positive effects of what happens when a woman accepts an assignment of refinement from God. Slowly God chisels away the ugly, the bad, and the even more ugly. And one day she finds herself choosing between what she wants most over what she wants now.

What commitment have you made that you're just not sure you can fulfill? It might be something simple or something complicated. But I want you to be a woman God and others can count on. I don't want you to quit your commitments. Because I know there's something unbelievable God wants to do through your life and in your circumstances. But will you be faithful "here" so He can get you "there"?

> A committed woman learns to choose what she wants most over what she wants now.

I want to introduce you to a woman in the Bible who has helped me understand the importance of completion. Her name is Ruth and she's a game changer.

Refinement Assignments

Okay, I know there have been a dozen books written and sermons preached on this woman. And I want you to know, **I know that.**

But we are not going to take this deep theological look at the book of Ruth. Instead, I want to show you what can happen when a woman follows through with her commitments. Not only does Ruth complete a hard assignment from God, but also Ruth is a woman God used to shape an entire generational line.

Do you want to break some cycles of defeat in your generational line? Do things ahead of you look a little impossible or hopeless? Are you having a hard time sticking with things all the way to the finish?

If you answered *yes* to any of these questions, then you too are a candidate for God to use to shift gears, change things up, and become the positive difference your situation needs.

Through Ruth's life I uncovered five habits, which led her to be a dependable woman. Throughout this book we are going to unpack her story, these five habits, and learn to apply these habits to our lives today.

The space between where we are and where we want to be is called potential. Ruth's story is filled with it and so is yours.

Really, Ruth had every right to quit. No one would have judged her decision to give up. And she could have justified the desire to quit more than once. But the first habit we are about to see lived out in Ruth, the woman who didn't quit, is this:

Habit One: She accepted
the assignment of refinement.

An assignment of refinement is a situation in life where we are given the opportunity to either go through it or grow through it. Typically these assignments catch us off guard; they come from a difficult relationship or life circumstance. Assignments of refinement are brought on by both controllable and uncontrollable situations. Meaning, sometimes we bring them on; sometimes they bring us on.

This fund-raiser situation started off as a conflict but ultimately became an assignment of refinement for me. And I bet if you look closely at your life right now, there's an assignment of refinement that is nearby.

Here's What Happened

The book of Ruth is sandwiched between two books of the Bible, Judges and 1 Samuel. It's only four chapters long. Four chapters! You can totally read that.

Ruth's story begins with a man named Elimelech and a woman named Naomi. They lived in a little town called Bethlehem, the same Bethlehem where Jesus would later be born. But there was nothing to eat in Bethlehem, and work was scarce. So Elimelech and Naomi packed up their crew (their two boys Mahlon and Chilion) and moved to a city called Moab.

Moab was filled with work and food, good things for people wanting to survive! But there were also some interesting situations with the people there called Moabites.

The Moabites worshipped a god called Chemosh. His name is about as complicated as my maiden name, Chevalier. But hello, my last name now is complicated too, Koziarz. I am apparently challenged with last-name complications.

Anyway, Chemosh was **not** the same god that Elimelech and Naomi worshipped, Jehovah. *Jehovah* is the one true living God. The worship of Chemosh brought on all kinds of awful things like sacrificing children and brutal sexual acts against women. It was a complicated religion, and the Moabites and Israelites typically didn't get along.

After Elimelech and Naomi lived in Moab for a little while, something really tragic happens.

> *Naomi's husband* Elimelech died, and she was left with her two sons. (Ruth 1:3, emphasis added)

Well, what on earth? The Bible doesn't tell us exactly what happened, but three verses into this story, Naomi's husband dies. While it's a terrible situation, Naomi still has her two sons, Mahlon and Chilion. Life carries on, and then something else interesting happens. The boys both marry Moabite women named Orpah and Ruth.

Hmm, Israelites married to Moabites. Two different faiths merging together. And it turns out that Moabite women used to seduce the Israelite men to lead them into sin. God actually struck those guys down dead because of their promiscuity and disobedience. Moabite women had a bad rep among the Israelites. So this is a curious situation merging together.

My husband and I started off our marriage in a similar way. Not in the *he was seduced by other women* way, but he grew up one faith, and I grew up in another faith. Needless to say, we had some bumps as we got going because of the differences in the way we were brought up to believe. So, I'm just guessing, but I imagine there were some snags in these marriages. Certainly there must have been discussions about faith. Maybe even some opposition.

But here's something I've learned about studying the Bible. Anytime we see something that has the potential for opposition, it's always an opportunity for God to reveal Himself.

And this concept is not just with the stories we study in the Bible. This is a truth for you and me today. All those refinement assignments where we feel so much opposition make us want to quit. They are indeed an opportunity for God to reveal His power.

> Opposition is always an opportunity for God to reveal Himself.

Moving past the interesting fact that these Israelite boys are now married to Moabite women, we see things get super complicated in this story.

> But about ten years later, both Mahlon and Kilion died. This left Naomi alone, without her two sons or her husband. (Ruth 1:4–5 NLT)

And boom. Just like that. Naomi's life and these two women's lives are forever changed. But for Naomi this was a worst-case scenario. Back in these days a woman's family was everything.

It wasn't like it is today where I can be a wife, a mom, a blogger, work part-time, be on the women's ministry committee, and wear all these hats that define me. A woman's family was it. So Naomi has in a sense lost her identity and is unable to provide for herself.

Naomi is left with so much heartache, bitterness, and confusion. The only thing she knows to do is go back to her hometown, Bethlehem. So Naomi tells the girls to pack their bags; they are moving out.

I've discovered most of the time when we go through a difficult situation, our natural instinct tends to be to *flee to the familiar.*

> When we walk through difficult situations, our natural instinct is to flee to the familiar.

Familiar Is Comfortable

There is something for each of us that provides comfort. This is why we have this thing called "comfort food," and we crave it when life feels out of control. My comfort food is my mom's chicken noodle casserole. It's the unhealthiest thing you've ever seen: egg yolk noodles, cans of chicken, cream of chicken soup, milk, and cheese. And on top? Crushed-up potato chips! But I will literally crave it when I feel like life is spinning out of control.

According to the American Institute for Cancer Research (AIRC), one in ten Americans said they gained weight in the months after the 9/11 attacks on the US. The time our country felt the most out of control, people fled to something that felt familiar to them, food.[1]

There are other things people do to feel comfortable during hard situations. Some people find familiarity through retail therapy or vegging on the couch with old movies. Sometimes we even go back to old relationships because they just feel comfortable.

But fleeing to the familiar is risky for a woman who wants to stop quitting. Because victory is often found in the most unfamiliar and uncomfortable places.

> Victory is often found in the most unfamiliar and uncomfortable places.

Naomi is fleeing to the familiar, Bethlehem. But this

is a new place for Orpah and Ruth. It's different. Strange. Scary. Unfamiliar. They both start off accepting this assignment of refinement and decide to go with her.

But not everyone who initially accepts the assignment of refinement sticks with it all the way. Trust me, I know.

The Quit List

I've pretty much quit everything.

You think I'm exaggerating?

I'm not.

Back in January 2014, I was asked to colead an online Bible study of the book by Lysa TerKeurst called *Made to Crave*. It's a book to help women (and men) overcome their addictive behavior.[2] And we may have had just a "few" ladies join us for this online study. A few as is in forty thousand! Holy smokes.[3]

For this study we were going to be specifically focusing on weight loss. So there before thousands of women, I declared on video teachings that this time it was going to be different. That THIS time I was going to make myself healthy. THIS time was it.

And it was "it" for about eight weeks. Then, over the next few months, the Bible study ended and life settled in. My girls got incredibly busy with their activities. My husband's company got stressful. Work got busy. And then, because we thought we didn't have enough going on, we decided to buy a fixer upper FARM. **Y'all, a fixer upper faaaaarrrrmmmmm.**

Like for real, what were we thinking? More on this later.

But a few weeks ago when I stepped on the scale to evaluate my progress, the scale said, "You quit." "You gave up on this." "You didn't see this thing through."

Nothing like thousands of women watching you fall flat on your quitting face. Not that I felt their judgment; they were the most gracious community ever, but my defeat made my heart sad. Because who wants to lead forty thousand women to a finish of defeat?

But defeat isn't just something I've struggled with recently. It seems like I have struggled with giving up on my commitments my entire life.

- As a little girl I quit the soccer team because, well, it was just boring.
- In middle school I quit many of my friendships because they were just drama.
- In high school I quit my health and went through an eating disorder.
- My first year of college I quit my purity.
- I've quit jobs because there was conflict.
- At least a dozen times I've tried and quit at getting the Koziarz crew on a monthly healthy eating meal plan. *Frozen pizza it is.*
- I've quit diet program after diet program.
- I quit trying to quit caffeine.

- Multiple times in my marriage, I've quit trying.
- When people get on my nerves, I quit caring about them.
- I've quit work-out programs because they got too hard.
- My laundry piles scream, "SHE GAVE UP!"
- I resigned from the PTO because PTO moms make me break out in stress hives.

And I've tried to quit motherhood at least a dozen times. But for some reason no one will accept that resignation. But I've wanted to quit. Like right now. As I'm typing these words, one of my little crew members is banging on the door begging me to stop typing and look at her outfit.

And since we bought this fixer-upper farm, there's a slew of esthetic quirks around the house. And the door to my office is one of those places; it's missing its doorknob. So she's sticking her mouth through the doorknob hole and screaming how unfair her life is and what a terrible mother I am because I will not stop typing and look at her outfit.

Hand to forehead. Please, someone give me a pink slip.

Looking back on my life, I realize just how much I've quit. And it's painful to think about how many opportunities I have missed out on because I gave up so easily.

Sometimes my quitting has had little effect on my life. But

> Sometimes quitting appears to have no effect until we take the time to reflect.

there have been other times it's created a tremendous over-flow of issues. As I look back over that list of things I quit, there were many, many results to those decisions.

What is one thing you've quit in the past five years that you are looking back on today and realizing you should not have quit?

As I look over my quit list, it's no wonder my husband felt like I wasn't someone he could count on. I haven't been. And the harder the assignment, the more likely I am to give up.

Maybe you've picked up this book because you can relate to this feeling of there being too much in front of you that looks impossible. Or maybe you feel like the 42 percent of my blog readers I polled who said their biggest struggle with God was falling into the same patterns of defeat over and over.

But more than anything, I'm guessing you are picking up this book because you have something inside you that needs to feel success. We live in a culture today that is con-tinually dumping defeat on us. The constant comparisons on social media remind us we are not good enough, we are not the best, we are not liked, and our ideas are stupid compared to others.

Can I just affirm for a moment those feelings you have? I really believe it's one of the reasons I quit things so often. Sometimes I have this messed-up perception of what it means to complete something for God. I too get caught up in the deceptive picture that completion means everyone loves what I've done and cheers me on the entire process.

Remember, refinement assignments are made up of both controllable and uncontrollable situations. Sometimes we bring on the hard places ourselves; others times life just seems to dump on us. But no matter what you want to quit today, no matter how hard or impossible it feels, I'm asking you this question, "Will you let this place refine your life to make you a stronger woman?"

I'm finding, as we begin accepting this assignment of refinement, there will not be a lot of people in our corners cheering us on. People just don't like to RSVP to these parties.

Naomi, Ruth, and Orpah found themselves in a horrible, refining situation. And at this point in the story, they are alone. There is no one guiding them through this or giving them a how-to manual. But so far they have said yes to the assignment of refinement. Except, for one of them, that's about to change.

Note from Nicki: At the end of each chapter, you'll see something called "Make It Stick." These are the quotes I want you to remember the most from each chapter. I've also got some questions for you to answer. We'll call these the *To Be Honest* questions, or if you want to be all trendy, #TBH. I challenge you not to skip over these because this is where the challenging stuff happens.

━━━━ Make It Stick ━━━━

Victory is often found in the most unfamiliar and uncomfortable places.

A committed woman learns to choose what she wants most over what she wants now.

Opposition is always an opportunity for God to reveal Himself.

━━━━ To Be Honest ━━━━

1. What are a few things on your quit list?
2. Where is your "flee to the familiar" place?
3. What is an assignment of refinement you are going through or have gone through?

2

Refinement Redefined

How many times would it take for someone to tell you *no* before you quit? For me? Not that many.

But for my husband? He never takes no for an answer. EVER. Which is why we now live on the Fixer-Upper Farm.

It all started because we knew we needed to move out of our suburban neighborhood in the little historical town we lived in. Not because we didn't like our house or our girls' schools but because things got really complicated with our home owners' association.

Those TV shows where people are being threatened and harassed by an HOA, which is led by individuals who seem to have a bit too much time on their hands? Yes, that.

They weren't after us because we didn't keep up our yard or paint our shutters an HOA-approved color. We did those things well and according to their guidelines. Really it was because of the HOA's increasingly strict new rules about my husband's work truck and trailer. He frequently needed to have both at our house while he was working on jobs. We tried our best to honor the regulations, but sometimes we just felt like the HOA was out to get us.

Like the time a woman sat in her car in front of our house taking pictures of my husband's truck. Or the guy on the HOA board who used to walk past our house every single day. The certified letters and the fines. *Too far.*

If you can't beat 'em, join 'em. If you can't join 'em, MOVE.

I was nervous about trying to find a new house in our area because this was an established community with little turnover. Bottom line: there were few houses for sale, with a lot of aggressive people after them.

Because of this, we started what would be a long dramatic house-hunting search. After several rounds of offers, counteroffers, and rejected offers, I started feeling hopeless.

One morning I opened up my computer and began to do my normal Internet search to see if any new houses in our area had come up for sale. And this intriguing listing I had never seen before popped up.

> We often discount what God is doing because we are determined to go our own way.

After getting excited about the potential of this property, I looked closely at the zip code and realized this property was WAY out of our much-loved community. I quickly assumed this was a search error and moved on.

As my day progressed, I couldn't shake that property out of my head. When my husband got home, I pulled it up on my computer to show him. It was basically a small version of our dream house with one added feature . . . *a farm!*

We kept pulling up the listing and looking over it closely.

Finally we decided we'd just "drive by it" to see what it was all about. We piled our girls into the van and drove and drove and drove. Past the city limits and past the comforts we had known for so long to a place where all you can see for miles and miles are farming fields.

A side road with a for-sale sign eventually greeted us. Slowly we drove down this bumpy, long gravel driveway, which was lined with these beautiful, old, majestic giant oak trees. Eventually we came around a curve. And in the middle of a big open field, lined with more crepe myrtles than I had ever seen, sat this little white house with black shutters.

I looked at my husband's smile and listened to the shrieks of my girls saying, "It's a farm! It's a farm!"

But the closer we got to the house, the more clearly we realized why the house was priced so affordably. It was a HOT MESS. And I'm talking weeds six feet tall, broken fences, overgrown bushes, a green nasty snake-infested pool, a building that smelled like someone had died in it, and a slew of other issues.

And that was just the outside!

It was obvious the property had been abandoned for some time. Yet there was something so intriguing about the whole place. When we stood looking out over the cow pasture, the trees seemed to sway as if they were saying hello to us.

But the shrieks of thrill from our girls suddenly turned into shrieks of fear as we saw a huge black snake slither across the sidewalk. Back in the car they went! The #farm-life was not #theirlife.

I was a little weirded out too and headed back into the van. But my Kris just kept looking at this property like there was some type of vision he was seeing. I took a deep breath and said, "I just don't know if we are in the season of life to take something like this on. But gosh, this is our dream, isn't it?"

He nodded his head. Our dream tangled up in one fat mess. A bigger mess than we could have imagined . . . EVER!

Don't Stop on Six

My pastor once gave a message titled "Don't Stop on Six." It was based on the story in Joshua 6. After six days of circling the city one time, Joshua and his army had to march around the walls of Jericho seven times on the seventh day. What if his army had stopped on six, given up, and gone home?[1]

It was one of the most inspiring messages I've ever heard on not giving up on something God has set before you!

And thank goodness Kris and I had heard this message because we may have quit the Fixer-Upper Farm dream if we hadn't.

After a lot of prayer and consideration, we committed to begin the process of purchasing the property. We knew there would be a lot of headaches ahead, but we were up for it.

And so began what seemed like the most complicated house-purchasing process on the planet. I kid you not, **six** different times we prepared for closing on the property, and each time something happened to stop it.

One time the closing was cancelled because of something that didn't pass inspection. Another time it was because of a fine "red line" with our loan and the fact that the property was a foreclosure. This red-line issue also led to us putting out a few thousand dollars for repairs without the assurance we would actually get the house. And a few other times it was because of paperwork or just something crazy. It was an assignment of refinement for sure.

Trying to buy a complicated farm and start a completely different life with your husband will give you plenty of opportunities to "purify your weaknesses" with each other. I don't think a day passed in that season when we weren't arguing over the phone with each other about something. It was so stressful, and we were getting close to the school year starting. Our kids needed to be settled!

Even the people who were closest to us during this season thought we were nuts to keep going through this. They were straight up getting on my nerves with all their, *"We just think you should consider other options."*

But we had committed to this process. We accepted the assignment of refinement. And while quitting this dream was an option, we knew there was more at stake.

It's Not My Favorite

Habit One of the woman who doesn't quit is:

She accepted the assignment of refinement.

Of all the five habits, this might be your least favorite. It's my least for sure. Not because this habit isn't a good one but because this is the hardest habit to actually live out. Which is why it might be the most important.

Refinement has so many meanings and definitions. According to the wise Google it means *the process of removing impurities or unwanted elements from a substance.*

When I think about refinement, I think about how we respond to hard and messy. For women who are being tempted to quit, there are many hard and messy things we find ourselves wading through. Some hard situations we bring on ourselves. I don't want to excuse us out of the wrong decisions we make.

But I believe **how** we walk through the assignment of refinement may determine our next assignment. I became really challenged by this idea one day when I read:

> For I consider that the sufferings of this present time are not worth comparing with the glory that is going to be revealed to us. (Rom. 8:18)

In this verse Paul (the author) gives us a word of wisdom and comfort about walking through hard things. While it may seem our present circumstances are unfair, ridiculous, and even wrong, there's a perspective of a coming glory.

> How we walk through an assignment of refinement may determine our next assignment.

If we quit, we might miss the opportunity to see God work in and through a difficult situation. And for Naomi, Ruth, and Orpah, it's come to this defining place.

Stay with God

I don't know what exactly happened on this journey to Bethlehem, but Naomi changes her mind about these two girls coming with her.

> She said to them, "Each of you go back to your mother's home. May the LORD show faithful love to you as you have shown to the dead and to me. (Ruth 1:8)

Perhaps the sight of these girls reminded her too much of the pain she had in her heart. Or maybe Naomi realized they would face difficulties ahead and didn't want to drag them through it with her. Whatever the reason, Naomi tells these girls that there is still hope for them and they too should **flee to the familiar.**

It's not an easy sales pitch for Naomi to convince these girls to go home. But finally Orpah agrees. She kisses Naomi good-bye, and with tears streaming down her face, she begins her journey home. And we never hear about Orpah again.

Orpah flees to the familiar.

But Ruth refuses to leave Naomi. She has fully accepted this assignment. And she begins to have this dramatic dialogue with Naomi.

> But Ruth replied, "Do not persuade me to leave you or go back and not follow you. For wherever you

go, I will go, and wherever you live, I will live; your people will be my people, and your God will be my God. Where you die, I will die, and there I will be buried. May Yahweh punish me, and do so severely, if anything but death separates you and me." (Ruth 1:16–17)

Are you picking up on the same tone I am with this girl's words? Her words are passionate, dramatic, and **desperate**. Somewhere along this journey things have changed for Ruth. She cares nothing about going back to her old ways, her old god, and her old family.

Maybe she has experienced the power of Jehovah.

Maybe she can't bear the thought of going back to her family.

Maybe she's clinging to the only ounce of her husband she has left through Naomi.

Or maybe, *just maybe*, God had stirred something so big inside Ruth she can't bear the thought of not seeing it through to completion.

Here's what I know about desperate situations: they can either lead us to a greater dependence on God, or they can cause us to detour away from God.

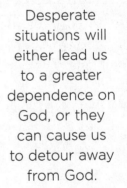

Desperate situations will either lead us to a greater dependence on God, or they can cause us to detour away from God.

So I have a question for you, *What makes you desperate?*

- With my health, will it take a discouraging diagnosis from the doctor to make me desperate enough to make major changes?
- In my marriage, will it take my husband telling me he's leaving me for me to become desperate enough to put forth the effort I know it will take?
- With my hopes, will it take me watching someone else live out my dream to make me desperate enough to pursuit it with all my might?

Am I desperate enough to become a woman who follows God through an assignment of refinement? With tears in my eyes, I wrestle with these words because some days I'm not really sure.

I get way too comfortable with this cycle of failure in my life. I tell myself there's always tomorrow to start over. But time seems to keep on marching. And life seems okay. So maybe I don't have enough desperation to really change.

But just like Naomi, Ruth, and Orpah, none of us are promised anything beyond this moment right here. Time is short, friends; the days don't go on forever. And we don't have forever to complete the God dreams and plans within us. It's such a complicated process, but if we can learn anything from this first part of Ruth's story, maybe it's just to *stay with God*.

When Naomi saw that Ruth was determined to go with her, she stopped trying to persuade her. (Ruth 1:18)

Stay with God when it's good.
Stay with God when it's bad.
Stay with God when it's easy.
Stay with God when it's hard.
Stay with God when you're confused.
Stay with God when it's clear.
Stay with God when you're lonely.
Stay with God when your community is thriving.
Stay with God when you want to quit.
Stay with God when you're driven to succeed.
Stay with God.

Before You Move, Hold On

I don't know everything Orpah had running through her mind during this defining moment. She made the decision to go back with little hesitancy. The Bible tells us she had tears in her eyes, but it doesn't seem like Naomi needed to do much to convince her to leave.

I've been an Orpah—confused, lost, and not sure how I could possibly stick out a hopeless situation. I've taken the comfortable path, and I cringe when I think about the things I have potentially missed on the path of refinement. All because I chose to turn back.

Because I know the end of the story, I know what Orpah is about to miss out on, and it makes me so bummed. I mean, maybe she went back to Moab and found a lovely man and rebuilt her life. But nothing can compare with what God is about to do through Naomi and Ruth.

If we move too quickly during assignments of refinement, we could miss what God has the power and the potential to do.

The reality is most of us want to just skip over assignments of refinement. There's this disillusionment in our minds that to stay with God means it will be easy, clear, and comfortable. It's a nice idea to believe following God means everything will just fall into place. The Bible doesn't tell us staying with God will allow things to turn out like we thought they should. However, it does say no matter what we go through there is nothing but an unending grace from God.

> If we move too quickly during an assignment of refinement, we could miss what God has the power and potential to do.

Indeed, we have all received grace after grace from His fullness. (John 1:16)

So maybe before we make that decision to quit an assignment of refinement, we need to

> When we stay with God, we stay with grace.

pause and ask for grace. Because God's grace is defined as unmerited favor. Meaning, He's with us and for us even in the hard situations. Grace can pull us through any hard circumstance. Grace to stay, grace to overcome, and grace to let our desperation become dependent on Him.

Thoughts, Words, Actions

Occasionally one of my three daughters will come home from school in what I call womp, womp mode. It's the mode where everything has gone wrong in her day, she has no friends, and life is just pitiful. Sometimes me just buying the wrong brand of cheese can send one of them into this quick downward spiral.

And I'll just be honest. Most days I don't want to hear it.

If their bad days are really serious, of course I listen, care, and comfort them. But my girls have a good life. They have good friends. They have more than most people in the world will ever dream of having. I just don't have a lot of mercy for the woe-is-me-I-didn't-have-the-right-brand-of-cheese days.

So we have a little saying in our house when their stinkin' thinkin' starts to take over:

Thoughts become words.
Words become actions.
Actions become reality.

When they can see absolutely no good in a situation and start speaking "death" over it, I will quote this to them.

And they will quote it to one another, and sometimes they quote it to me.

The Last Straw

We were driving down the road when our realtor called. It was the sixth time we had tentatively scheduled the closing for the Fixer-Upper Farm. And of course, there was a problem, and our closing was rescheduled **again.** I threw the phone down and said to my husband who was seated next to me: "This is NEVER going to happen. We just need to give this thing up. That's it! I can't take it anymore."

And wouldn't you know, there was this little eight-year-old girl sitting behind me who piped up her little voice and said, "Nuh-uh Momma. Thoughts become words. Words become actions. Actions become reality. Don't you speak that over our farm!"

My husband smiled and nodded his head. I was eating my own words. This season of learning to wait, to trust God, and to believe was starting to mess with my thought process. It was refinement mixed with stress, anxiety, and fear. A quitting formula for sure.

It required a transition in my thinking, my prayers, and my belief. I had to make this shift while not knowing the end of the story.

I know this whole buying a farm drama thing may sound incredibly juvenile in comparison with the "real" problems of this world, but trust me when I say the Lord used it to work in my life. I assure you there will be *all kinds* of seasons of refinement as we work to become women God and others can count on. Later you'll hear more about the seasons of refinement I've gone through that were no laughing matter.

Some seasons of refinement will cause us to look back and laugh. Others may continue to produce an ache felt deep in our spirit for many years to come.

Maybe one day Ruth got to a place where she was able to look back on a few places of this horrible tragedy and smile about the refining process. But where we are meeting her right now, there's nothing funny.

Her thoughts could have easily become clouded. But she seems to have so much clarity in her decision to stay. There's not a hint of hesitancy to flee. It makes me think her desperation was creating a dependence on God.

Thoughts are powerful when we are walking through refinement assignments. While we will never be able to control all the events that happen or hard situations we find ourselves wandering through, we have control over our thoughts.

For as he thinks in his heart, so is he. (Prov. 23:7 NKJV)

This book isn't about to turn into a Positive Thinking 101 class, but I do believe in the power of putting the thoughts of God into us. Thinking as He thinks of us:

> "For My thoughts are not your thoughts, and your ways are not My ways." This is the LORD's declaration. (Isa. 55:8)

Understanding how the Lord views us is foundational to viewing these seasons of refinement as assignments from God. There's something He wants to shift in us, teach us, and fulfill through us. As shown in Isaiah, we are different from God in both our natural thoughts and actions. In order for the shift to take place, we must spend time learning His thoughts and His ways. We have to allow Him (and His Word) into those deep places, our thoughts. The places where no one goes but Him.

Our thoughts become the words we speak. The words we speak become the actions we take. The actions we take determine our steps toward the future.

God is not a puppet master controlling our every move. The decision to stay with Him through our thoughts, words, and actions will always be ours.

> God is not a puppet master controlling our every move. The decision to stay with Him through our thoughts, words, and actions will always be ours.

Redefine Refine

I used to resist this word *refinement*. I felt like figures of authority would toss it out when they were trying to correct some type of bad behavior in me. But the more I've come to understand refinement, the more I've come to see it is an assignment from God.

Some words we can compare to the word *refinement* are *improve* and *touch up*.

These words make me feel like going through hard things and ending well is possible. Redefining refinement with these two words has helped me when I feel like quitting because things are getting messy or hard.

Refinement Redefined Word One

IMPROVE

A question to ask: Rather than making me quit, how can this refinement assignment help me improve *my* character?

A thought to consider: It's important for us to have a healthy perspective on what in our lives needs to be improved. We will never arrive at perfection. Heaven help us if we think we do.

And for women who have the tendency to quit, we have to be willing to look at the areas in our lives that need some improvement. Hard situations are a great place to see things in us that need to be changed.

Albert Einstein once said, "Once we accept our limits, we can go beyond them." I love this quote because it reminds me how important it is to see where I've limited my perseverance. Once I get there, then I can take the steps needed to improve my character to help me push past my wanting to quit.

I can choose to improve my thoughts, my words, and my actions once I admit they need some tweaking.

A verse to hold onto: A man who endures trials is blessed, because when he passes the test he will receive the crown of life that God has promised to those who love Him. (James 1:12)

Refinement Redefined Word Two

TOUCH UP

A question to ask: Do I need to quit this refinement assignment, or is there something I just need to *touch up* with a little more effort, grace, or understanding?

A thought to consider: Goodness, I mess up all the time. I say things I shouldn't say. I have thoughts I shouldn't have. I doubt when I should trust. I quit things I shouldn't quit. And yet God is always there, dabbing more and more grace on my soul. He doesn't quit me; He just keeps "touching up" the places of weakness in me.

As we walk through assignments of refinement, there are times we just need a touch up, a slight twist in our attitude or response. It's letting our lives truly become a mold of His Word in and through us.

A verse to hold onto: Yet LORD, You are our Father; we are the clay, and You are our potter; we all are the work of Your hands. (Isa. 64:8)

It Happened

Finally, after waiting for three months to close on the Fixer-Upper Farm, Kris and I held our breath as we walked into the lawyer's office for closing.

A big fancy table, cushioned chairs lined with upholstery nails, three pens, and a bottle of water awaited us. I was shaking I was so nervous. I had this horrible feeling something else would happen at the last minute to make the deal fall through. My thoughts were screaming, *It's not going to happen Nicki!*

But I'm working on this thought thing. I really want to improve my thought process. So, embracing this assignment of refinement, I popped open my phone and grabbed one of the quit-quitting verses I'd been trying to memorize (the entire list is found at the back of the book!).

I am sure of this, that He who started a good work in you will *carry it on to completion* until the day of Christ Jesus. (Phil. 1:6, emphasis added)

I took a deep breath and touched up my thoughts with truth. According to this verse, what God ordains, He sustains. It requires me sticking through the process with Him all the way.

As the lawyer sat down, anxiety overwhelmed me because he looked concerned with one of the documents. Tears started to swell up in my eyes as I thought about the deal falling through again. My soul just couldn't take it.

But our realtor fumbled through his file and pulled out the information they needed. The lawyer smiled, handed us our pens, and we signed our lives away for the next hour.

It was hard, it was stressful, but it happened. We didn't quit. We saw the whole thing through, and now we were holding the promise, the vision, the dream we dreamed.

And you will too my friend. It might not be a fixer-upper farm, but there is a beautiful *something* ahead for you.

The assignment of refinement will typically catch us off guard. And the level it pushes us toward quitting is extremely high. But you are going to see Ruth live out this habit more than once in this book.

Will you accept the assignment of refinement?

━━━━━ Make It Stick ━━━━━

We often discount what God is doing because we are determined to go our own way.

Desperate situations will either lead us to a greater dependence on God, or they can bring fear and anxiety resulting in greater uncertainty.

If we move too quickly during an assignment of refinement, we could miss what God has the power and potential to do.

To Be Honest

1. What is an assignment of refinement you moved too quickly through?
2. Have you ever been so determined to go your own way you realized later how much you missed what God was doing through that assignment?
3. Do you feel like you are desperate enough to make changes?

✓ **Habit One:** She accepts the assignment of refinement.

Habit Two:

Habit Three:

Habit Four:

Habit Five:

3

Quitzilla

Habit Two: She follows through with her commitments despite how she feels.

My friend Melissa and I used to work out together. I say _used to_ because, remember, my name is Nicki, and I've quit everything.

Anyway, I signed up for this boot camp with Melissa in one of my I'm-so-desperate-for-change stages. My thighs were getting gigglier, and my muffin top was no longer sucking in, despite all the fancy undergarments I bought.

For the first few weeks boot camp was a really good thing. I felt great after I worked out, my muscles were stronger, my clothes were fitting better, and I had a new circle of friends working toward the same goals.

But like a lot of things I begin, my commitment to boot camp began to waver. I'd still show up most days, but I was well on my way toward quitting. The excuses began to trickle in, "Oh, I have to get my daughter to school early." And, "Whoops, my alarm clock didn't go off," but really I had just hit the snooze button five times. The times I did show up, my efforts were pretty lame. I found all kinds of shortcuts through the workout and spent most of the time whining about how sore I was.

One Thursday morning Buck, our boot camp teacher, was in a pretty bad mood. Normally he was super encouraging, but on this particular morning I felt like he was fed up with me. He probably was; I would have been fed up with me too.

Buck was making me do all these dreadful things like jumping off boxes, lifting ridiculous amounts of weights and burpees. *Oh my word . . . the burpees.*

Toward the end of the workout, fumes were starting to pop out of my head. I felt like Buck was being extra hard on me. The last part of our workout that day was these things called planks. Planks are basically putting your entire body weight on your elbows and holding your body up for as long as required. *R-i-d-i-c-u-l-o-u-s.*

Buck had instructed us to hold our plank for a certain amount of time; I can't exactly remember what the time limit was. But it was an eternity, *I promise.*

So in my head I counted the plank out, and Buck counted according to his stopwatch. But for some reason my count and Buck's count were very different. When I finished the count in my I head, I dropped to the ground. But Buck screamed at me to get back up!

With wide eyes I looked at my friend Melissa who was right beside me and said, "Did he just YELL at me?" She confirmed, "Yep." *Well then.*

We finished the first set, and then it was time to do another set. But by this point my entire body was shaking. I didn't have much strength left in me.

The next set started, Buck started his stopwatch, I started counting in my head: *1, 2, 3, 4 . . .*

Again, *in my head,* I was done about three seconds faster than Buck's stopwatch. And so when I dropped to the ground, he yelled at me for the second time to get back up.

Well, I did not get back up. In fact, I started crying. I had to excuse myself to the bathroom because the tears just kept on coming. I felt like a mortified wimp.

Here She Comes, Quitzilla

I know Buck wasn't trying to humiliate me; he was doing what I paid him to do, push me. But in that moment, on that day, I just couldn't take it anymore.

I got in my car to drive home and called my husband in tears. I went on and on about how ridiculous this whole boot camp thing was. I had been working out for weeks and was not seeing the results I felt I should see by this time. Working out like this first thing in the morning was just flat-out stressful. By this time my mom guilt was overwhelming because our kids were going to school without me saying good-bye.

My entire perspective on this boot camp had drastically changed. So my poor fed-up-with-my-whining husband said, "Well, then just quit."

AND I DID.

I became quite the Quitzilla: furious, fed up, and fast to walk away.

How dare Buck yell at me like that! This boot camp is so stupid; it's not working anyway! What a waste of money and my time! Ugh!

Later that day I e-mailed Buck and told him I wouldn't be back to the boot camp for a variety of reasons. He was disappointed in me and told me he was still going to have to charge me for the entire amount.

Whhhaaatttt? This made me even angrier.

I paid in full vowing never to step foot back into that boot camp. Besides becoming a Quitzilla that day, something worse happened inside me. I quit my health. All the weight I lost came back on, and working out was not a priority anymore.

Here I sit almost two years later typing these words, wondering what I would look and feel like today if I hadn't given up so easily.

Honestly, I'm tired of her, this woman, who quits everything and continues to stay in the cycle of failure. She hardly completes her assignments each day, and she gives up effortlessly. The banner over her life is exhaustion. And she's this woman God and others can't count on.

This Quitzilla, *me*.

But through Ruth's example I've had a small taste of what happens when a woman decides she's going to become someone who follows through with her commitment. She has the potential not only to change generational lines but to infuse her world with blessing.

The scent of this woman has stirred a holy fire in me.

She is able to look into the future with confidence because she is determined to become the vessel for what she has been created to do. She's not tossing pennies into the wishing well of life. Her focus is contagious, and she has the ability to stick with things long enough to master them.

She understands that the days, weeks, months, and years aren't here forever. And the passions within her have the ability to become forgotten daydreams.

Does she sound impossible?

Good.

Because on her own, she is.

But there is one thing this woman believes with all her might: what seems impossible is just the peak of a miracle with her God. He's got more than enough power to overcome any quitting process. And if He is for her, then truly nothing shall stand against her.

> With God what seems impossible is just the peak of a miracle.

I don't want to be a Quitzilla, and I don't think you do either. It's time to write new endings to the stories from our past that haunt us. It's time to learn new patterns so we can begin experiencing victories.

She accepts the assignment of refinement was the first habit of the woman who doesn't quit. We've accepted it, and now we are ready to roll our sleeves up and dig into the second habit:

Habit Two: She follows through with her
commitments despite how she feels.

I've Lost That Loving Feeling

I know we live in a world that screams we should follow our gut, our instinct, and especially our feelings. It seems like many of us are never fully devoted. We keep one foot in and one foot out of commitments. And the right quitting formula, mixed with uncertain feelings, will lead us to abandoning our commitments.

Somehow we have to learn more times to stick things out past how we feel. Momentary feelings will always try to convince us to forfeit our faithfulness.

> Momentary feelings will always try to convince us to forfeit our faithfulness.

Can I be perfectly honest with you? Writing a book about not giving up might have been the dumbest idea I've ever had. My marriage, my job, my blog, my volunteer position at church, my healthy eating plan, and my cleaning routines are just a few of the quitting struggles I'm facing today. Currently I have commitment after commitment I want to quit and, in some cases, I have quit.

I even told my husband after writing about this boot camp story, I really don't like myself. I feel like such a wimp and want to quit writing this chapter. *Why do I quit things so easily?*

Truly I wish I had this lovely bow to tie around this story and tell you I went back to that boot camp, apologized to Buck, and worked hard to finish my goal. But I didn't. And there are a slew of other stories you'll read through this book of times I didn't follow through.

You've lost that loving feeling with your commitments? Me too. But ultimately we have to own this but decide that commitment has nothing to do with our feelings.

It's taken me time to understand this Quitzilla that lives deep in me. Why does she give up so easily? What are the things that trigger her to quit? What are the quitting patterns of her past? Where have her feelings led her astray?

> Change is possible, but it comes best when we've put our feelings to the test.

Let yourself wrestle with these questions. Change is possible, but it comes best when we've put our feelings to the test.

Stop Blaming

I used to think my patterns of defeat came from people saying I couldn't do something. If I felt the slightest tinge of disbelief from someone when I shared a hope, dream, or plan, I'd quit.

I'd also sulk in the misery of quitting if I felt someone could do something better than me. And internally I'd blame that person for my giving up. Bottom line, this is some messed up thinking, right? My feelings have led me away from commitments multiple times.

But something shifted in me when I came to accept the truth that my defeat comes from **my thoughts** and **my reactions.** Usually we are not defeated by what others say or do to us; ultimately we are defeated by what we say and do to ourselves. I have allowed my commitments and decisions to be driven by how I feel for too long.

The Quitzilla in me has convinced me to do everything based on how I feel.

When it feels hard, just quit.

When it feels messy, just quit.

When you don't feel like it's going your way, just quit.

When you feel like it's not going to work out, just quit.

There's a Quitzilla in each of us. She might be quiet today, but pushed hard enough, she'll come out swinging. Emotions, circumstances, and feelings will always attempt to dictate our level of commitment to the tasks before us.

I've also seen how many Quitzillas have deep wounds from past failures. They have tried and failed repeatedly. Every Quitzilla has a voice of doubt that is always competing with the voice of Truth. And she feels like something is always trying to detour her route.

Been there. Done that. Writing the book about it.

We can put that Quitzilla away and begin to restore what she has stolen from us.

One of my favorite Bible verses is Joel 2:25: "I will restore to you the years that the swarming locust has eaten, the hopper, the destroyer, and the cutter, my great army, which I sent among you" (ESV).

This promise of restoration for the repentant people points toward grace. Grace for yesterday, grace for today, and grace for tomorrow. It is never too late for God to change and restore the brokenness in our lives that impacts those around us. No matter how hopeless it looks.

We have an enemy of our souls whose goal is to kill, steal, and destroy. Satan would love for you and me to believe it's over and it's never going to be as we hoped. He may be the initiator of every quitting desire, but we have to own our part in allowing our feelings to control our actions.

There is something to be said about a woman who follows through with her commitments, despite how she feels. There's strength, honor, and God's glory on the other side of remaining steadfast.

As we pick back up with Ruth's story, we're going to see a situation that quite possibly could have made it difficult for Ruth to feel like sticking with her commitment to Naomi.

We are going to see the second habit of the woman who doesn't quit fulfilled by Ruth:

> Feelings don't have to be what fuels our faith.

She follows through with her commitments despite how she feels.

She's Just Mad

Naomi didn't seem to carry any sense of hope about the future. The woman was ticked. I mean, you know you're mad if you want to change your name to "bitter."

Naomi and Ruth continue on this journey to Bethlehem. Everyone is so excited to see Naomi. But she immediately tells people to call her *Mara,* which means bitter.

> "Don't call me Naomi. Call me Mara," she answered, "for the Almighty has made me very bitter. I went away full, but the LORD has brought me back empty. Why do you call me Naomi, since the LORD has pronounced judgment on me, and the Almighty has afflicted me?" (Ruth 1:20–21)

I am in no way minimizing what happened to Naomi. While I have walked alongside people who have lost their children and husbands, I personally have never walked through it. But changing your name to "bitter" is pretty extreme.

It's easy for me to sit behind a computer and type words to ring with the loveliest southern drawl, "We should just all be like Ruth, full of hope." But here's what I'm most afraid of: I think if I were to walk through a situation like this one, I would tend to be more like *Naomi* than Ruth.

Bitterness has the potential to bring a perspective that because life has not panned out as we hoped, we've lost the hope for a good life that is before us. And living our lives feeling bitter will definitely make us not feel like following through with our commitments.

Can you imagine what this was like for Ruth? She has already traveled such a long distance with a depressed woman. I'm sure their little road trip playlist didn't include Pharrell Williams's "Happy."[1] And now they arrive in this new town, and the first words out of Naomi's mouth are filled with hopelessness and despair. I'm amazed Ruth was able to stick out this commitment because that right there would have made me want to quit.

Somehow Ruth's perspective needed to rise above all the feelings. She was deeply wounded too. She had lost everything too. But she isn't letting her feelings drive her commitment.

Bitter Quitter

The other day I was driving one of my daughters to a commitment she had. And the entire way there she told me all the reasons she didn't want to go. Most of the reasons were a little juvenile, like she wanted to go sleep over at a friend's house. But at the core of this not wanting to follow through with her commitment, I sensed a sting of bitterness toward the leader of the event.

I asked her a few questions about the leader to get a better understanding of the situation. There was some tension because the leader wasn't setting the best example, assigning the majority of the tasks on my daughter. When my daughter insisted she was dropping out of this commitment if the leader didn't do A, B, and C, I knew I had my own little Quitzilla on hand.

The leader had made some mistakes, but my daughter had let things settle inside her for months. And now she was just fed up and ready to quit! But quitting when we are angry or upset almost always leads to regret.

> Quitting when we are angry or upset almost always leads to regret.

As I read Naomi's words about wanting people to call her another name, I could tell bitterness had been settling inside her for a long time too. I wondered if one day she would look back on this initial conversation with old friends and have some regret.

Prolonged bitterness will bring out a Quitzilla faster than any other quitting symptom because it has an overflow of effects. I did some research on the effects bitterness can have on our bodies, especially how we feel. And I found out lingering bitterness can actually make you feel physically sick.

There's a term for prolonged bitterness, it's called PTED (posttraumatic embitterment disorder). People experience symptoms of anxiety, depression, and rage. I have even heard that it can also affect their immune system and organ function.[2]

This is serious stuff. Which may be why God gave us Ephesians 4:26:

> Be angry and do not sin; do not let the sun go down
> on your anger. (ESV)

Many times our emotions would have us believe our only options are bitterness or quitting. Unfortunately neither option encourages us to follow through despite how we feel. That day I explained to my daughter the need for her to persevere despite how she felt in that moment. I also gave her permission to confront the hard issues she was facing with this leader. Tasks were not being divided up equally, and my daughter was carrying most of the weight. She needed to respectfully address these frustrations.

If she truly was not enjoying this commitment anymore, she needed to evaluate it from a distance. Not when she was angry or upset but when she could look at the situation with clarity. More than anything my daughter just needed to know someone was in her corner and saw what was really happening.

Maybe that was one of the reasons for Naomi's dramatic entrance into town. She wanted to be sure everyone knew what she had been through and how awful it was. And it was awful, extreme, and horrible. But was this bitterness going to ruin her for good?

Let me get in your corner today. What is that thing that is making you feel so incredibly bitter and pushing you to quit? Don't let bitterness mess up this process for you. Ask the Lord to bring it to the surface right here, right now.

I haven't seen exactly what happened to you, but there is a God in heaven who sees everything. He knows how unfair life has treated you, how wronged you felt by that person, and how broken you feel about that one situation.

And because He has seen it all, He so honors the process of letting go of our bitterness.

> Let all bitterness and wrath and anger and clamor and slander be put away from you, along with all malice. Be kind to one another, tenderhearted, forgiving one another, as God in Christ forgave you. (Eph. 4:31–32 ESV)

Life has dealt many of us unfair cards. And when we feel like we've been treated unfairly, bitter roots have the potential to spread. Maybe we don't have PTED, but if there's a sting in your soul, there's potential for bitterness to be produced.

To become women who follow through despite how we feel, we must take these fragile places in our souls to God. He knows. He hears. He sees. He desires to journey with you as those places, experiences, or people surface in order for healing to take place. The process of not allowing bitterness to slip in and ruin our lives will look different for each of us.

Some of us may need to have conversations that bring closure to conflict. Maybe a few of us need to apologize for something we have done. I need to stop replaying and analyzing events in my head; I'm so bad about hitting the repeat button on what went wrong.

According to the Mayo Clinic, letting go of bitterness can lead to:

- Healthier relationships
- Greater psychological well-being
- Less anxiety, stress, and hostility
- Lower blood pressure
- Fewer symptoms of depression
- Stronger immune system
- Improved heart health
- Higher self-esteem[3]

All things that will definitely help us feel better. I love when modern medicine further demonstrates what we are told in Scripture!

Ruth and Naomi had a different perspective at this point in their story. Their feelings led them through different processes. And bitter Naomi almost missed it, but Ruth was in a posture of looking for the treasure in the trial.

I Can't

To become a woman who follows through with her commitments despite how she feels, we are going to have to eliminate these two words "I can't" from our vocabulary. The moment these two words roll off our tongues, defeat is soon to follow. When we say these two words, "I can't," what we are really saying is, I don't *feel* like I can do this.

You are breaking into new territory. People following all the way through despite how they feel isn't common. And it's going to feel strange as you let your feelings shift from driving you away to driving you to stay.

So go ahead and get rid of all these I can't's:

I can't start this business because I don't *feel* like I have what it takes.

I can't lose weight because really I don't *feel* strong enough to do it.

I can't stay married because I *feel* like he will never change.

I can't accept their apology because I *feel* too hurt.

We waste a lot of time convincing ourselves of what we can't do. But God's Word spends a lot of time telling us (with Him) we can not only do a lot of things but all things.

I am able to do *all things* through Him who strengthens me. (Phil. 4:13, emphasis added)

With Him, we can do hard things:

He gives strength the weary and *increases the power* of the weak. (Isa. 40:29 NIV, emphasis added)

And with Him we can do impossible things:

But Jesus looked at them and said, "With men this is impossible, but with God *all things are possible.*" (Matt. 19:26, emphasis added)

What have your feelings convinced you that you can't do?

We never see Ruth bringing an excuse or an "I can't" to this situation. She knew remaining steadfast would pay out even when she didn't know the end of the story.

──────── **Make It Stick** ────────

Momentary feelings will always try to convince us to forfeit our faithfulness.

Change is possible, but it comes best when we've put our feelings to the test.

Quitting when we are angry or upset almost always leads to regret.

━━━━━ To Be Honest ━━━━━

1. When was the last time you felt like a Quitzilla?
2. Is there any area of your life where you are feeling like you have become a bitter quitter?
3. What are the "can'ts" in your life? Begin reframing those "can'ts" to identify the how.

4

Determined

It was one of the worst mornings I've ever had. The alarm went off late; my three girls were in sass-a-frass mode; Herman, our slightly famous pug, pooped all over my rug; the well on our Fixer-Upper Farm froze (again); and a mouse had apparently died in our walls. So on top of all the chaos, there was some awful smell floating through the air. Oh, and our heat downstairs broke. Fun morning.

Flustered from this horrible start to the day, I finished getting ready in my room away from the chaos. In the quiet of my bathroom, I got dressed and went over to the bathroom sink to put my contacts in. At least this brought some normalcy to my morning. Or so I thought.

The night before I had stopped by a convenience store to pick up some contact solution on the way home from my middle daughter's swim practice. And of course, they didn't carry the normal brand of solution I used, so in a hurry I grabbed the best looking box. (I know, I'm such a marketing sucker consumer, *pretty packaging . . . ooohhh*.)

We got home, I went to get ready for bed, and I opened up the box. There was some crazy contraption for the lenses to go into. I mean, it looked like it belonged in the Stone Age so I was like, *Whatever. I am not using this.* I poured the solution into my normal lens case and scooted off to bed.

Well, after my no-good-horrible-morning start, I was in such a rush to get to work. So I quickly popped my left contact lens into my eye. But a few seconds later I was screaming as loud as a two-year-old who had just gotten their bag of Skittles taken away. There was a burning sensation in my eye that was so bad I couldn't even open my eye.

I have one of those ~~not so~~ incredibly helpful teenagers who knocked on the door and said, "Are you like okay, Mom? I mean, calm down." As she opened the door, she quickly realized this was QUITE a situation and immediately called for her daddy to come. By the time Kris arrived in the bathroom, I had gotten the lens out, but my eye was blurred and burned.

I expected him to be as fearful as I was of what had happened. But instead of him wrapping me up and scooting me off to the doctor, he simply said, "You okay now? I gotta get to my first job site of the day."

I said something fairly ugly, let out an exasperated scream, and slammed the door in his face. I found my way to the sink and flushed my eye out with water, but I could tell this was pretty serious. So I called a local eye doctor's office to see what I needed to do; they told me to come in immediately.

After a careful examination the doctor said I would be fine, but I had some burn damage. He also explained that this was apparently something that happens often to people who use this certain brand of contact solution I had purchased. He tried to be as kind as possible, but I could tell he was rather flustered that I hadn't taken the time to read the BIG RED warning label across the bottle.

The warning label that said you need to use the lens contraption **provided** or the solution won't work properly. Because if you don't, it's like dropping straight peroxide into your eyes.

Oh.

Oops.

He gave me some drops for my eyes, which provided immediate relief. But I left that office feeling like a complete red-eyed fool.

When I got home, half the workday was done. I didn't have time to go into the office like I was supposed to. But I still had so much work that needed to get done.

And on top of that, I just felt like no one in the world cared about me. My husband's reaction toward this situation hurt me. I know he wasn't intentionally being mean, and he really did need to get to his first job site of the day.

Still, sometimes we (women) just need a little TLC. And when we feel like no one cares about us, we can feel like we want to withdraw from the world.

Every part of me just wanted to call out sick for the rest of the day and lie in bed and watch Lifetime movies. But I knew in my e-mail in-box there were urgent e-mails that needed a response, I had a virtual meeting to run with my team, and I had assignments with deadlines. And darn, I was trying to be this woman other people could count on. I had a choice. Let my feelings dictate my day or follow through despite all that had happened.

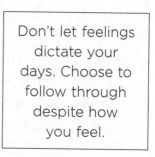

Don't let feelings dictate your days. Choose to follow through despite how you feel.

So, despite how I felt, despite my circumstances, I got to work. I'm determined to live out our second habit: She follows through with her commitments *despite how she feels.*

I had to continually pause and ask God for strength to push through. But that day I saw God do something miraculous. Everything on my to-do list somehow got accomplished in a shorter time than it ever did.

I also discovered something incredibly valuable about myself that day. With God I can follow through with the commitments I've made, despite how I feel. I'm seeing how

He thrives in the business of showing strength through our weakness.

I saw the power of this again yesterday. I was handed a volunteer assignment at church I felt less than thrilled to do. Normally I would have put it off until the last possible second because *I didn't feel like doing it.*

But I'm learning my follow-through can't be dependent on desire. Just because something isn't fun or exciting is no longer an excuse for me. I knocked the assignment out in just a few minutes and was thankful to be someone who could be trusted **past** the fun assignments.

For sure there will be times when circumstances are beyond our control and prevent completion of a task. Things like jury duty, sickness, and family emergencies happen without notice. But those exceptions are not what I'm referring to here. I'm talking about the places where our fleshly weakness numbs our commitment level. It's the place where apathy steps in convincing us it's just not worth it to follow through.

According to Dictionary.com, *apathy* is defined like this: "absence or suppression of passion, emotion, or excitement."[1]

So often things start off exciting—new job, a promotion, a new relationship, or a leadership opportunity. These commitments seem to begin with an element of fun. Maybe you get to go buy some cute shoes for your new job or read some incredible books on leadership for your new role. Or maybe your parents or friends take you out for dinner to celebrate your new assignment.

But then it's time for the work to start. The deadlines are looming, the cute shoes hurt your feet, and the boss isn't as nice as he was during the interview. And it just doesn't seem as awesome anymore.

Those things that once made you feel so alive now make you hit the snooze button one too many times each day. If you are finding yourself feeling incredibly apathetic today, it's okay. I've been there too. And so has everyone who is reading these words.

But change is coming. There are a dozen things you don't feel like doing today (probably even reading this chapter!), but you have to press through because there is something for you on the other side of this.

I don't know what exactly that something looks like for you. But I know it's going to be powerful. I believe the people who feel the weakest have some of the greatest God assignments to complete. Even if it doesn't seem like it, the boundaries of your current assignments are within the strength of God.

> The boundaries of your current assignments are within the strength of God.

First, Find Hope

We were out of options. The day the sheriff's car pulled into our driveway, I knew what was coming. After a series of unfortunate events, things had gone from bad to worse to hopeless.

Her friendly, official, sheriff smile did nothing to relieve the emotional discomfort of this dreadful moment. The neighbors peeked through their blinds to see what was happening.

As she handed me the papers, I took them with tears in my eyes.

Looking at the baby in my arms and the toddler peeking out from behind me, this kind woman genuinely said, "I'm sorry."

"Thank you," I whispered, as I slowly closed the door.

I sat down on our stairs and read through the official documents. Elaborate lawyer terms, forceful sounding laws I didn't understand, and words bolded in dark ink conveyed the dreadful news: "You must vacate the premises within thirty days."

Foreclosure.

It was unwanted and unavoidable. It felt shameful and embarrassing. And the foreclosure of our first home was an aching process of letting go.

The carefully painted mustard-yellow walls—I would miss them so much. How would I survive without the daily afternoon playdates with my neighbor and her children?

And what about all those hot dog dinners my husband and I ate to save pennies to buy this sweet home?

So much was about to be taken from us. Just like that.

I didn't understand why God would allow us to walk this humbling road. We had trusted Him. Why hadn't He provided?

Any hope I had left in God faded fast. It wasn't something I could muster back up on my own. No, I needed others to fill the gap for me.

I learned during this devastating season, when our hearts become grounds of broken dreams, we may need to turn to the hope others can help us find.

As my mom came over and helped me pack our boxes, she told me better days were coming. I found hope. When our little girls ran around our new rental property with excitement and wonder, I found hope. As my husband helped me paint the walls in our rental to a color I could live with, I found hope.

Ruth did this so well. She followed Naomi all the way to Bethlehem. When they arrived and began to settle in, she had experienced a great deal of Naomi's bitterness. Things weren't looking hopeful for the future. She must have known she needed to do something different in order to keep her hope alive.

Ruth asks Naomi a question . . .

Ruth the Moabitess asked Naomi, "Will you let me go into the fields and gather fallen grain behind someone who allows me to?"

Naomi answered her, "Go ahead, my daughter." (Ruth 2:2)

At this point in Ruth's story, hope would come in the form of being able to provide for her and Naomi. Ruth knew she needed to get to work and find that hope. When we don't feel hope, we have to find hope.

Gathering the leftover grain was a right widows had in the Jewish community (Lev. 19:9–10). The poor and widows would come behind the wheat gatherers and pick up any leftover grain left on the edges of the fields. This wasn't an easy job. And it wasn't a highly favored position.

I wondered if Ruth felt scared? After all, this was brand-new territory for her. A new town, new people, and now a new job. Since bitterness was in their home, Ruth decided she was going to join others gleaning hope in the form of grain. Even if that meant entering a field as a foreigner.

I feel like that right there is a message for someone. There are times when we just have to get behind people and pick up the leftovers. Whose dropping joy by you today? Pick it up. Is there a little bit of faith someone is leaving with you? Take it. Has someone overflowed with peace in your life today? Receive it. There's hope in the leftovers people leave all around us. Like Ruth we must take that initial step and choose what feels unnatural.

Ruth doesn't know this but she's about to discover that hope is where our miracles begin.

"So that having been justified by His grace, we may become heirs with the hope of eternal life." (Titus 3:7)

When we choose to surrender our lives to Jesus Christ, we have hope for today and hope for tomorrow. There is always a filter of hope to put our lives through when we *stay with God.*

The Filter of Hope

Hope is not a wish; it's a holy confidence that faith will give us the strength to push through every hard and trying circumstance. An English historian once said, "Discontent and disorder are signs of energy and hope, not of despair." So if things are looking a little rocky, it's okay.

> Hope is a confidence that faith will give us the strength to push through every hard and trying circumstance.

Since I find myself being naturally drawn to giving up on things when they feel all out of control, maybe I just need a slight perspective twist. You too?

Hope-filled perspectives will always be the greatest prescription for a potential Quitzilla. And sometimes we just need to put our feelings through a little filter. Below is a three-step filter you can put your situation through the next time things feel hopeless. I hope it helps you as much as it's helped me in my journey!

The Filter of Hope

1. Recognize we cannot control the things that happen to us, but we always can control our reaction.

Ruth and Naomi were completely out of control when it came to the tragedy they were walking through. There was nothing they could do about it. But Ruth was in control of the fact that there was something she could do once they arrived in Bethlehem. She knew something in their lives needed to change. Her reaction was to find work.

Write down the things you can control right now and the things you can't.

2. Appreciate what you have.

When things are looking hopeless, it becomes so easy to lose sight of the blessings we already have. Naomi's perspective was clouded by her bitterness, but soon she will understand more fully and see Ruth as a blessing. Are you able to see the blessings in your life? If not, do you have someone to help you identify blessings in your life? People seem to be generous to help us see things through their perspective. Don't be afraid to ask someone for help.

Make a list of five things that are a blessing for you right now.

3. Give it some time.

Remember Orpah? Naomi's other daughter-in-law who went back to her old family, her old god, and her old ways? Unlike Orpah, Ruth gave it some time. She didn't make a drastic decision in the midst of high emotions. You'll see the benefit of this as we continue to work our way through Ruth's story.

Ask a friend to hold you accountable with this.

When we put our feelings through this filter, it will help us step back and look at things

> Feelings fog our focus. Hope filters failure.

with a clearer perspective. Feelings fog our focus. Hope filters failure.

It's Not in the Wiring

I'm really not wired to be one who follows through despite how I feel. And I have proof! It came in the form of a StrengthsFinder's test result.[3]

Have you heard about this book and tool? It's truly a life-changing evaluation of your personality that will tell you what your strengths are. We as a society are always encouraging ourselves to work through our weakness, but this book teaches you to work with your strengths.

One of my top strengths is ideation. Bottom line: I have ideas and have a lot of them. This doesn't mean they are all good ideas, but it means they are there. I've learned how to leverage this strength in building up God's people. So don't be surprised if you get an e-mail from me one day with a BIG idea for your life.

A person with the strength of ideation may have the great idea but may not execute the ideas well. I am awesome about saying, "Here's the idea! Now go find someone else to make it happen." And sometimes seeing a project all the way through is grueling. It's because in my head I see it completed, but implementing the plan is different.

Maybe you don't have ideation as a strength, but you still struggle making commitments that feel beyond you. I want you to know, you are completely normal.

The question I've wrestled with as I've let this second habit sink inside of me is, how do we follow through with our commitments despite how we feel?

Is it by being disciplined? Is it by being focused? Is it a supernatural power only some people receive?

Maybe it includes one or more of those things to a certain extent. I'm starting to realize it has more to do with how I perceive the situation.

What's in Your Head?

I have such a great community on my ministry Facebook page. I love those people and the way they connect, pray, and challenge one another and me.

But Lord help me if I post something and it has a typo in it! I mean, within moments I will have a *dozen* alerts of my typo. Most of the time they are gracious alerts, but every now and then a snarky comment gets thrown in there.

What I can't seem to figure out is how I check my posts for typos multiple times, but I still make the dumbest mistakes. Like misspelling the simplest word in the English language, *the*.

A few days ago I was reading an article about why writers tend to miss their typos. Basically the article said what's on the screen is competing with the version that is in our head.[2]

So in my head I spell the word *the*: T-H-E. However my screen shows I hit the "h" button twice. So I really typed THHE. But that's not what I see because in my head I wrote THE.

Makes sense, right? We see things in our head a certain way, but often in reality they appear very different. Ever get lost while driving because you *thought* you knew the right way to go? Or have you ever gone to the grocery store and bought everything except the one thing you came for?

Seeing things in my head a certain way happens a lot to me. My husband has this joke that I think **everything** costs around $5 and takes about five minutes. And when things end up costing a lot more time and money than that, I'm often shocked.

Like the time I asked him to knock down a wall in our kitchen on the Fixer-Upper Farm. It seemed simple to me. *Boom. Pow. Now. Wow!*

But in reality it meant demolition, rewiring outlets, drywall mud and dust for DAYS (oh my word, the drywall dust), and a lot of time on my husband's part.

It's not just with typos, driving, projects, or money this happens. In my head . . .

- The scale says a certain number, but then the actual stepping on the scale moment, reveals a different number. I'm shocked and have a hard time figuring out what went wrong with my eating/exercise plan.
- My relationship with my friend is just fine. But her irritated text message to me tells me something is different. I'm surprised, and I can't seem to figure out what I've done wrong.
- I am someone others can count on because I say yes all the time. Then, while sitting in a meeting without my completed assignments, that sick feeling washes over me. I realize I've taken on too much. I'm confused because I don't know when it became too much.

In my head I know what I want my life to look like. Getting there often leaves me feeling frustrated. What I've come to understand when I don't get the results I want or expect is the passion for what I'm doing becomes almost nonexistent.

In this place I find myself wanting to quit because I feel tired, angry, or upset.

Quitting is made up of both big and small defining moments.

The day we hand in that resignation letter, make the phone call, sign the divorce papers, put the soda back into the fridge, or stop showing up to our commitments are all huge defining moments. Looking back, I can clearly see those moments with my quitting journey.

But what I hardly ever see are those little moments I make in the process that lead to these big defining moments:

The negative attitude that starts to slip in:

I wouldn't do things this way. I think my way is much better.

The unrealistic perception of how much time is really available each day:

"I'd love to help you with this project!" said over and over and over.

This idea that every Monday is a start-over day:

I'll just eat this cookie today and start my diet over again Monday.

The doubts I let myself believe:
You can't really do this.

Failing to follow plans, a schedule, or a routine:
I just like to go where the wind blows each day.

Evaluating what's in our heads isn't the fun part of our journey, but it is a necessary step to becoming one who follows through on her commitment despite how she feels.

I know some things about you based solely on the fact that you picked up this book. You are exhausted with the cycle of defeat in your life. You want more. You desire a fulfilling life. You are tired of quitting. You have a dream, a purpose, or a desire that has yet to be fulfilled. You are afraid you are going to miss it if you don't stick it out this time.

I get all those thoughts and reasons. Neither I nor anyone else can sell you a three-step program to get you to where you need to be. But together we can learn how to evaluate our feelings so they don't drive our commitment level.

Make It Stick

Don't let feelings dictate your days. Choose to follow through despite how you feel.

The limitations of your current assignments are within the strength of God.

Hope is a confidence that faith will give us the strength to push through every hard and trying circumstance.

─────────── **To Be Honest** ───────────

1. What is competing in your head with the reality of what is happening in your life right now? We have to figure this out in order to keep moving forward. List two things you want to quit.

   1.

   2.

Now think about where you are in your quitting process. Have you already decided you don't feel like doing it so you're not? Or are you willing to recognize the need to follow through, despite how you feel?

✓ **Habit One:** She accepts the assignment of refinement.

✓ **Habit Two:** She follows through with her commitments despite how she feels.

Habit Three:

Habit Four:

Habit Five:

5

This Dream Is on Fire

Habit Three: She stays open to the movement of God.

What would you do if your dream were on fire?

Like, literally.

Run? Scream? Stand there with your mouth dropped open? That's basically what I did.

When Kris and I purchased the Fixer-Upper Farm, we had big dreams. We were going to pinch our pennies to buy a tractor, some cows, and plant ourselves a bountiful garden.

Because that's what farmers do, right? Right. Never mind the fact that we are first-generation farmers and have no idea what we are doing. We try.

But there's nothing like a mishap with the septic system to throw your bank account out of whack. Makes you have to become extra resourceful.

And becoming resourceful is the mantra of the #farm-life. My creative ideas and my husband's resourcefulness make us excellent at this.

For example, Kris rebuilt the fence around our back-yard by piecing together broken pieces of the old fence. It was a long, grueling process, but the fence looks amazing and cost us little.

And since the gravel driveway was a mess, he built this gravel road level thing that he hooked up to our riding lawnmower. *(I wish I was all-fancy with my farm equipment terminology, but I'm not. Gravel-road-leveler thing it is.)* Cost him almost nothing to make it. It works great too!

We've done pretty well with making do with what we have. Doesn't mean we don't drive past other farms out here and drool over their barns and tractors.

#ThingsINeverThoughtIWouldSay

But we get by, most days.

We've also met some really resourceful people who help us when we get stuck on things. Like my friend Phyllis.

She's a few decades older than me. And she's from Ghana, so she's got this really impressive accent. Everything she says sounds *magnificent.*

Phyllis has taken great interest in our Fixer-Upper Farm. She's a master gardener, so she's got all the tips and tricks. And because she is so wise, when Phyllis tells me I need to do something on the Fixer-Upper Farm, I listen.

Which is how I first learned about Back to Eden gardening. In case you're not into gardening, I won't bore you with all the details about how a Back to Eden garden works. Basically it's doing things in a natural, organic way.[1]

After many conversations and research with Phyllis, I was convinced this was the direction we needed to go with our farm. I had a plan. I ordered all our seeds and plants, we prepped the garden area, and we waited for spring.

The Fire

When you're a girl who quits everything, procrastination is definitely something you struggle with. And so the first spring on the Fixer-Upper Farm came, and I got really busy with my speaking/travel season. The Back to Eden garden planting priority kept getting bumped.

Each time I'd pull out of our long, gravel driveway, I'd look over to the area we had prepped. I kept telling myself I had a few more weeks to get the plants and seeds into the ground.

Those weeks passed, and the garden area became full of weeds! And then the smart gardening people said one more week left to plant for this season.

It was now or never for the garden.

But this weed situation was going to set us back several hours of work. So I started to do some research on how to naturally get rid of weeds *quickly*.

Pinterest has always been a great go-to resource for natural garden ideas. I saw a lot of Pinners had pinned this article about burning weeds out of the garden. Fascinated by this concept, I told my husband about it, and he agreed this idea would save us tons of time!

My husband and a project that involves fire is one he's always up for. So I sent him out there with his blowtorch, and I got all our seeds and plants ready for planting. He had the best time lighting those weeds on fire and was careful to make sure the fire was completely out once the weed was dissolved.

After five strenuous hours in the garden, we had successfully gotten rid of all the weeds, planted three hundred corn seeds and a bunch of other things. This burn-your-weeds thing was efficient gardening gold.

Exhausted, we went to bed that night with dreams of corn stalks and tomato plants dancing in our heads.

The next morning I was fumbling around the kitchen trying to find something to relieve my body of all its aches. Clearly my back was letting me know gardening did not agree with it.

I realized I had left the pain reliever medicine in the car so I walked out our front door. And as soon as I opened the door, my heart trembled and my mouth dropped.

To my right there was smoke everywhere, and our first little Fixer-Upper Farm garden was encased with smoke! In my black-and-white striped pj's and flip-flops, I ran to grab the garden hose. I was so mad! I could not even believe this was happening.

Apparently the burn-your-weeds Pinterest idea was a bit more complicated than it appeared on the pretty little graphic I pinned. Oh the weeds were gone, but, uh . . . so was pretty much everything else. While we had thought the fire was completely out, it wasn't. Obviously. The hot smoke must have continued to smolder overnight creating this scorching mess.

Sighs. Sometimes I feel like I start to take ten steps forward only to take fifty back. *Can you relate?*

Quitting becomes incredibly tempting when we make really good efforts and they literally seem to go up in smoke. But when we accept our assignment of refinement, follow through with our commitments despite how we feel, then we can begin to live out the third habit of the woman who doesn't quit:

She stays open to the movement of God.

Learning to stay open to the movement of God is going to be tricky for those of us who tend to want to hold on to our plans. But there's a process to uncovering the plans of God. You have some things in mind for your future, but so does God.

Many plans are in a man's heart, but the LORD's decree will prevail. (Prov. 19:21)

As we learn how to stay open to His movement in our lives, we are going to see some things happen we could have never dreamed of.

It Just So Happens

After discussing it with Naomi, Ruth heads out into the field and starts working. And she finds herself in the perfect situation.

So Ruth left and entered the field to gather grain behind the harvesters. She happened to be in the portion of land belonging to Boaz, who was from Elimelech's family. (Ruth 2:3)

Now let's stop RIGHT THERE. This part of Ruth's story makes me so happy. This was really good news that Ruth found herself in this field. There was a lot of potential in this field, potential way beyond just picking up leftover grain. And do you see the part of this verse that says, *"She happened to be . . ."?*

Ruth remained steadfast throughout her entire journey. And now we are beginning to see how God's leading her every step into something special.

> God gives favor for small steps of obedience over big empty promises.

Staying open to His movement means we stop trying to determine where our commitments ultimately lead. It's putting one foot in front of the other slowly but surely.

Let's just imagine for a moment what could happen:

You don't feel like going to help out in the nursery. But you accept your assignment, follow through with your commitment, and rock the babies.

It just so happens that baby's momma comes to know Jesus that day, and a family is forever changed by the grace of God. You are now part of their story.

You don't feel like going to the gym. You're tired; it's been a long week. But you accept your assignment, follow through with your commitment to get healthy, and go anyway.

It just so happens this workout pushes you to a level that sustains you for weeks.

You don't feel like completing that project for work, but you accepted this assignment so you follow through anyway.

It just so happens this was the project your boss was waiting to see you finish to give you that promotion.

This **just so happened** moment is huge for Ruth. It's when she encounters Boaz *(spoiler alert!)*, this man who is going to change everything for Ruth and Naomi.

You know what I love about our God? I just never know what He's up to! We can't predict all the good things He wants to do in our lives. But we know His Word tells us He honors those who keep their word.

When you make a vow to God, don't delay fulfilling it, because He does not delight in fools. Fulfill what you vow. Better that you do not vow than that you vow and not fulfill it. (Eccles. 5:4–5)

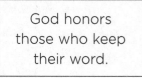

God honors those who keep their word.

I believe God is looking for some people today who will keep their word, follow through despite how they feel, and leave the results to Him. And on the opposite side of this type of obedience is blessing.

When You Don't Know What God's Doing

I will not pretend to have an answer for why something can just go up in flames when we've remained committed. We come up with plans, we seek council, and we work hard, yet sometimes it seems like it still doesn't pay off.

Maybe you've never had a garden catch on fire, but you've had some fires to put out . . .

- You make a decision to honor and respect your boss only to turn around and find out he said something untrue about you.
- You start a new workout program and hurt your knee after the second workout.
- You decide to stay committed to your marriage only to discover your husband has cheated again.
- You become determined to get out of debt and pay extra on your credit card each month. But a few weeks into your payoff plan, you find out you owe the government thousands of dollars in taxes.

On the other side of every problem is a solution that works. But on the other side of every solution is the potential for another problem. When a woman struggles with quitting, it seems like she has a lot of problems. There's always *something* trying to detour her route.

Remember, our third habit is:

She stays open to the movement of God in her life.

What this means is we are going to have to accept the fact that sometimes things aren't going to turn out as we had hoped.

Even if we try with all our might.

Even if we plan and plan and plan.

Even if we have all the determination in the world.

If I had to sum up this third habit in one word it would be *surrender*. But I realize that word *surrender* sometimes seems so unattainable and overused. It's like our pretty little Christian word we give people when things aren't going as they hoped: *"You just gotta surrender, honey."*

But let me tell you, when I was standing out there with the garden hose in my black-and-white pj's, I didn't feel like staying open to anything God was doing. I was mad. And now today, after I finish writing this chapter, I have to go back out to that garden and start from scratch. I am *less than thrilled* about this.

But help me, Jesus, I cannot write a book about not quitting and give up on that garden! And you, my friend, cannot read a book about quitting and make decisions to quit right now either.

When the fires come, and they will, quitting will always seem to be the best escape route. But if we take a few more steps, show a little more effort, and put a few more seeds in the ground, maybe, just maybe, we will start to see something beautiful happen as we see in Ruth's life.

> Whatever we are trying to overcome will most likely turn into our greatest opposition.

What's on Fire for You?

Use this space below to write out what your "fires" are right now.

_____

_____

Ruth is about to teach us something incredibly valuable about what it looks like to stick with a commitment, to follow through no matter what, and to stay open to what God is doing.

#HumbleBrag

Have you heard about the #humblebrag phenomenon that's happening across social media platforms? It's these status updates that make everyone wish they had a smack button. One where the person is bragging while trying to present themselves as humble. Everyone recognizes the false humility except for the person posting. Here's an example:

> I'm exhausted from my two-week vacation in Hawaii. I need a vacation from my vacation.

Really? Says the mom who's been up with a screaming baby for weeks. _Really?_ Says the professional who's working two jobs and still isn't making ends meet. _Really?_ Says the schoolteacher who gives herself selflessly to students all year long and can barely afford a pool membership for the summer.

We've all seen these types of social media updates, and they are so incredibly annoying. Like, just post your stinkin' beach pictures so we can virtually high-five your trip and carry on with your life. We do not feel bad for you!

As we pick back up with Ruth's story, she's out in that hot field working hard. Boaz has taken notice of her, and they are entering into a delightful conversation. Boaz tells Ruth she is welcome to come glean in his fields anytime. In fact, he doesn't want her to go anywhere else. He promises her security and safety there.

And Ruth is just overwhelmed by this man's kindness. She completely humbles herself, and Boaz actually begins to brag on Ruth! This is a #HumbleBrag I think you'll love.

> She bowed with her face to the ground and said to him, "Why are you so kind to notice me, although I am a foreigner?"
>
> Boaz answered her, "Everything you have done for your mother-in-law since your husband's death has been fully reported to me: how you left your father and mother and the land of your birth, and how you came to a people you didn't previously know." (Ruth 2:10–11)

Ruth didn't bring her plan, her agenda, or even her dream into the field to pick up leftover grain. She didn't have a picture of what God was doing. But as she walked into that field for the first time, crunched herself toward the ground, and picked up pieces of grain, she was open. Open to this field, open to Boaz, open to God.

Go Low, Stay Open

I was thinking of all the ways Ruth could have started off her conversation with Boaz. It could have included a bunch of whining and complaining, *Naomi is so bitter. This is hard work out here. I've done so much already. Boaz, can you just hook a girl up?*

But she went low. Like, kneeled down with her face to the ground low. And when she did, Boaz lifted her back up. Not literally but with his words. He tells her, *I have heard all the good things you have done. I see you girl; you are something incredibly special.*

You know, sometimes a girl just wants someone to notice her. But what we are seeing fulfilled through Ruth is described perfectly by Jesus later in Scripture:

> Whoever exalts himself will be humbled, and whoever humbles himself will be exalted. (Matt. 23:12)

Surrender and humility hold hands when we are staying open to the movement of God in our lives.

Surrender says: "God, even though I don't understand what You're doing through this assignment, I'm open to it."

Humility says: "Lord, I know the glory is on the floor. If no one but You sees this act of obedience right now, I'm okay with it."

I am 100 percent guilty of not living out true surrender/ humility. I want people to high-five my efforts all day long. We live in such a culture that cultivates this type of affirmation from the world. We blast our workout pictures, our healthy dinners, and our completed projects all over social media.

Sometimes we do this to inspire others, but if I were to guess, I'd say most of it comes from a place of just wanting someone to see what we've accomplished. And not only do I want someone to see what I've done; I want my efforts to lead to specific results.

> Surrender and humility hold hands when we are staying open to the movement of God in our lives.

It's Not Embarrassing

It took me awhile to understand the difference between humility and humiliation. All my life I've heard people say things about people who make mistakes like, "God's just trying to humble them." But humility that honors Him doesn't have to be brought from a place of humiliation.

The time I walked into a speaking engagement, slipped, and fell flat on my face in front of everyone, HUMILIATION.

But the time I called someone I really respected and was completely honest about something wrong I had said, humility. It was so hard, but I knew I was in the wrong. And the gift of grace I received on the other end of that call was a beautiful fruit of humility.

Humility isn't a place where God's trying to embarrass us. It's the place where God wants to show us how we desperately need Him in our lives.

This is a lifetime process. We will never fully arrive at this place. But I hope you see, like I did, how God can take a broken woman, who was working hard,

> God's not trying to humiliate us by humbling us.

and give her the affirmation she needed through someone else. Without her having to say a word. All because she was willing to *go low* and *stay open*.

God is working behind our scenes in ways we just can't know about yet. He is preparing the way in your life for His plans to prevail. But this is going to take some effort on our part.

Risky. This is how it's going to feel as we work through this habit. To put aside old habits and put new ones on isn't comfortable. Maybe it sounds exciting at first, but to follow through despite how you feel and stay open to what God is doing—it's tough.

But if we can really grasp surrender and humility through this process, we might be a little closer to victory than we originally thought.

There's No Formula

When I first started the book-writing process, I went through several conversations with literary agents. Everything I'd ever read or heard on writing a book said you needed a literary agent. So off I went in search of a literary agent.

But none of the agents I ever talked to seemed to mesh with me. Some wanted me to chase them, some I just didn't feel like they believed in me, and some just flat-out told me no.

Humility came whether I wanted it to or not. But would I be willing to surrender? Because a woman who stays open to the movement of God learns to do **both**.

One afternoon I was doing that comparison game in my head. I was sizing myself up to other first-time authors and started to quit the book-writing process. It just wasn't happening for me!

And I felt the whisper of God say to me, *What if I want your process to look different from everyone else's?*

I cringed. Because most days I wish there was a formula with God. I wish God would talk to me like the life coach podcasts I listen to; they just tell me how to do stuff. If I do *a, b,* and *c,* the end result should be *d.* Right?

Wrong.

Formulas are good for two things: *babies and math tests*. God has never fit into formulas, even as much as the Church has tried to put Him in them. He's mysterious. His ways are different. And He holds a picture of our life we cannot even possibly try to comprehend. So, why do we try to formulate God?

Over the past few years of this writing process, I have had to tell myself multiple times I was going to learn to stay open to what God was doing. And when I started to want to get all control freaky with God, I would remind myself of this Scripture:

> "For My thoughts are not your thoughts, and your ways are not My ways." This is the LORD's declaration. (Isa. 55:8)

I stayed low for a long, long time. There were many rejection letters, many other book ideas, and many tears. And do you know how this book you are holding came to be? Conversations and opportunities that "just so happened."

In this field Ruth "just so happened" to be with Boaz. The right place, the right time, with the right person. When I stopped fighting for a formula and fought for humility and surrender, then I saw God move.

> When we stop fighting for a formula and fight for humility and surrender, then we see God move.

I'm starting to understand how becoming a woman who doesn't quit means sometimes God just needs to take us through some stuff quietly. Where our agendas are laid down, there are no revealed plans, and no one is affirming us.

It's a secret place of surrender.

This third habit, staying open to the movement of God, looks like this: surrender, stay humble, surrender again, and then . . . get even more humble. If we do not give up on this process, in due time He will lift us up. Just like He did through Boaz with Ruth.

Humble yourselves before the Lord, and He will exalt you. (James 4:10)

When we learn to stay open to what God's doing, **then** He can do something special.

Then

Before we moved to the Fixer-Upper Farm, we lived in a little historic town, charming and full of life. Especially in the spring, with the mature dogwood trees and gardens in full bloom. There were several old houses that I'd love to look at on my daily drives. One in particular was a creamy yellow, craftsman-style house with a lot of character.

The owner of the house would sit daily on the front porch in his brown wicker rocker, gazing at the world as it passed by. Since he was there almost every day, I called him the town watchman.

But one morning my daily drive past the old house took a drastic scenery turn.

As I pulled around the curve toward the house, I noticed black smoke and orange flames shooting out of the upstairs window. No fire trucks or police yet; it was the raw scene of a fire with frantic people running around.

My heart sank as I slowly drove by. But what made my heart ache even more was what happened later that afternoon.

The fire trucks, police, and even the American Red Cross were gone. But there on the front porch, amid yellow caution tape and a red UNSAFE sign nailed to the corner post of the house, sat our town watchman. He was in his brown wicker rocker, seated for his daily assignment of town watching.

A man stood at the edge of his driveway on a cell phone. He looked flustered, angry, and as if he was trying to get our town watchman off the dangerous front porch. But there was no budging, no getting him to go anywhere. The look on his face screamed that this was his home, his post, and he wasn't leaving.

Our town watchman had a redefining moment that day. The house he called home was no longer safe. The porch on which he sat was now filled with rubble. Life as he knew it was about to change.

As I watched him sit on that porch, holding on desperately to what he had known, I could identify with the feelings his soul invariably worked through. As the days, weeks, and months passed, he will now categorize his life with words like, *Before the fire . . . or After the fire . . .*

Seems like no matter how much we don't want tragedies or painful experiences to define us, they still do.

- The rejection.
- The cancer.
- The loss.
- The divorce.
- The death.
- The depression.

As we travel through the afters of life, we will crave the moments of joy we had in the befores.

But God is teaching me something, especially when these hard things make us want to quit. While we cannot go back to the life we once had, we also don't serve a God who is a "once" God.

He's a "then" God.

- Jesus died. **Then** He rose (Luke 24:1–12).
- People were sick. **Then** Jesus healed (Matt. 14:14).
- Life feels desperate. **Then** Jesus straightens the path (Prov. 3:5–6).
- You were broken. **Then** God put you back together (2 Cor. 4:16–18).

Letting go of what is gone is painful, and looking toward what is ahead is sometimes hard. It's learning to stay open to God in the hardest sense. For Ruth this might have been the most difficult part of her process.

But Ruth was letting God be a *then* God, and she didn't even realize it. As she was in the midst of that conversation with Boaz, she was having a "then" moment with God.

Ruth followed through with her commitment to stay with Naomi, *and then God* led her to Boaz's field (Ruth 2:3, emphasis added).

Ruth surrenders her plans, her dreams, and even her hopes. *And then God* began to give her great favor as she "just so happens" to be in Boaz's field (Ruth 2:10, emphasis added).

Ruth falls flat on her face in humility, *and then God* lifts her up through Boaz's words of encouragement (Ruth 2:11–12, emphasis added).

I'm challenged to allow God to be my "then" God, and I hope you will be too. I want to trust God with these places that don't seem to make much sense right now. When life and dreams feel like they are on fire, they may be. But there's still something there for us when the fire cools down.

My friend Meg actually gave me some good news today. She's a farm girl at heart and knows a lot about planting gardens. She said the fire in our garden might have actually been a good thing. Sometimes a farmer will intentionally burn a field to improve the health of the field. It helps rid the soil of anything else that's growing to give the seeds the best chance to thrive. Yes, I still have to go out there and replant every single seed, but maybe it's not as bad as I originally thought. Maybe there's a better garden coming.

Make It Stick

God honors those who keep their word.

Surrender and humility hold hands when we are staying open to the movement of God in our lives.

When we stop fighting for a formula and fight for humility and surrender, then we see God move.

To Be Honest

Use the space below to write a "before" and "after" moment of your life. Turn it into a "then" statement. Use the Scriptures in the back of the book or throughout this chapter to help.

6

Take COVER

My husband and his mom danced to the Bette Midler song "Wind Beneath My Wings" (circa 1991) at our wedding. It was pretty epic. Not because they rocked the dance floor, but the look on my husband's face during the dance was *claaasssssic*.

First, my husband isn't really the dancing type. He's more the bob your head kinda guy. Second, my husband doesn't do mushy. And that song is nothing but mushy.

His mom's eyes were just leaking and leaking as they danced. But Kris's face just screamed, "Bette, why must this song go on so long?" He loves his mom. He just doesn't love the mushy dancing and mushy songs.

What is that man going to do? He has not one, not two, but THREE daughters he will probably have to mushy dance with at their weddings one day! *Poor man.*

Ruth's story is about to get a little mushy. For you hopeless romantics, you'll love this part. But I don't want us to get caught up in the mushiness and miss what I consider one of the most powerful sentences in this whole story.

In the last chapter we saw the great #HumbleBrag moment. Ruth's ability to stay open to what God was doing and go low was working in her favor with Boaz. He told her he saw how awesome she was, and Ruth never had to say a word.

And now Boaz offers Ruth these words of blessing:

> May the LORD reward you for what you have done, and may you receive a full reward from the LORD God of Israel, under whose wings you have come for refuge. (Ruth 2:12)

So sweet. But I want us to dig deeper into the part that says "under whose wings . . ." because there's nothing mushy about that part. This is the part I consider one of *the* most powerful statements in the entire book of Ruth. And understanding this statement will help us even more as we continue to unpack this third habit: She stays open to the movement of God.

What Are These Wings?

My feet have been going in the church doors since before I could walk in. I have sung all the songs about being under the wings of God; I have read all the pretty graphics with the Psalm 91:4 verse:

> He will cover you with His feathers; you will take refuge under His wings. His faithfulness will be a protective shield.

But you guys, can I just be honest with you for a second? Until almost a year ago, I really had no idea what it meant to take refuge under God's wings. I mean, it sounded like a nice thought, but I was totally clueless about what it actually meant.

So at first I wondered if maybe the Bible described God with having wings? Nope.

Then I wondered if it was referencing the angels that the Bible describes as surrounding us with protection. Nope. (I know, I just took us to a whole new level. Hold on, we're coming back down.)

Finally, I was like, WHAT ON EARTH ARE THESE WINGS?

So I did some research, and here's what I discovered:

The wings referenced in the Psalm 91:4 verse, as well as this one in Ruth 2:12, are referring back to something called *the ark of the covenant.*

If you knew the Bette Midler song I was talking about before, you are from an era where you've probably seen or heard of the movie *The Ten Commandments*:

"Let my people go!"

"Moses! Send forth My word."

"After this day you shall see his chariots no more!"

Oh, sorry. Back to Ruth.

Okay, so the Ten Commandments were the ten laws God gave Moses to give to the Israelites (Exod. 20). They were rules they needed to live by in order to please God. And they were tucked away in something called the ark of the covenant to be kept safe. Across the top of this box it had angel wings that spread across. It was called the **atonement cover**.

It might have looked something like this:

Here's how one source described the atonement cover:

The *atonement* cover was the lid for the ark. On top of it stood two cherubim (angels) at the two ends, facing each other. The cherubim, symbols of God's divine presence and power, were facing downward toward the ark with outstretched wings that covered the atonement cover. The whole structure was beaten out of one piece of pure gold. The atonement cover was God's dwelling place in the tabernacle. It was His throne, flanked by angels.[1]

Those wings **covered** the presence and power of God. Things have changed for us since the Ten Commandments were put into place for the Israelites. We no longer have to go to a "special place" to experience the power and presence of God.

And we no longer have a list of rules and regulations to follow for God to love us. Through Jesus, God invites all of us to live under this same type of covering in our everyday, modern lives. You can experience the presence and power of God in the carpool line with screaming kids, at the gym, with your husband, and at your job.

This is exactly what happened to Ruth. She was experiencing the presence and power of God in this field, whether she fully understood it or not.

God's been teaching me a lot about how to live under His covering. It started with that Back to Eden garden. The main secret to this all-natural garden is what you cover it with: wood chips.

The guy who came up with this gardening method explained it like this: When you walk out into the woods and you see the trees growing and thriving, do you ever wonder how they continue to grow without anyone tending to them? He said if you look on the floor in the forest you'll see it's covered with leaves, pine needles, fallen branches, and bark that has fallen off the trees.

The ground is **covered**, and it helps protect the roots so they can do what they are supposed to do best: to grow deep and spread.

He said this was the original plan God had for plants, that they would grow and thrive on their own. Over the years (maybe we didn't intentionally mean to do this), but we have messed up God's plant system. We now need all kinds of pesticides, special seeds, and unique soil to grow food properly.

I was so intrigued by this because whether or not you agree with the *Back to Eden* gardening method, the truth is, in order for us as human beings to thrive in life, we also need *cover*.

Most of us have clothes that provide our bodies with *cover* (thank goodness!). We live in houses that provide us with *cover* from weather and hungry, wandering animals. Blankets *cover* our beds so we can sleep better. If we don't *cover* our skin when we're outside in the hot sun, we'll burn.

And there are a dozen other things we could list that provide *cover* for us.

We know that coverings are important for us, but what about when it comes to living under the covering of God? How does that work?

Well, if we broke the word *cover* down, here's what we have:

C-O-V-E-R

And then, if we put a space between the letter *C* and the *O*, here's what's we'd have:

C   O-V-E-R

Do you see it? It says . . . *See Over.*

Really, living under the covering of God means we are asking God to "see over" our lives. But not just for the good, happy places. It's those hard places too, the places that make us want to quit because we don't understand what God is doing.

God sees over our lives by teaching us what His Word says. He also surrounds us with people who can speak truth to us and by showing us He can work through every circumstance if we'll trust Him.

But see, if I stop reading His Word, God can't teach me what it says. And when I isolate myself from others who love God, I can't be poured into. Or, if I am determined to make things happen my own way, I might miss what God has for me.

When we decide to come under the covering of God, there are three steps we take with our lives:

Step One: We admit how much we try to control things.

Step Two: We tell God we're open to what He wants to do in and through us.

Step Three: We stay in place under the covering of God, even when it's not making sense to us.

Which of these steps do you feel like you need to take most?

_____

_____

See-Over Prayers

In this process of learning to stay under the covering of God, I've been praying something called See-Over Prayers. I mentioned this before so we know there's no magic formula with God. We can't do *a, b, c,* and expect a perfect *d* result. That's not what these prayers are.

These prayers are really a way for me to communicate with God but also to remind my brain that I'm trusting God even when my soul wants to run. I keep them close by because almost every day I need to remind myself of one of these prayers.

See-Over Prayers contain two things: my problem and God's promise.

Usually the problem I'm facing has come from some form of wanting to be in control. And it almost always leads to my quitting patterns. I find there are three areas I constantly struggle with releasing control: my marriage, motherhood, and our finances.

These prayers help me release the results I want and push my heart to rely on God.

So here's what a See-Over Prayer looks like for me:

> See-Over Prayers help us release the results we want and push us to rely on God.

My Marriage

God, sometimes I feel hurt in this marriage. But I know that Proverbs 10:12 reminds me, "Hatred stirs up conflicts, but love covers all offences."

So, right now, I come under Your cover so that You will **see over** my words, my heart, and my marriage.

My Kids

God, I never know if I'm making the right decisions with my kids. I don't have the answers right now, but I know Proverbs 24:3 says, "A house is built by wisdom, and it is established by understanding." I am bringing my house under Your cover so You can **see over** the decisions I need to make concerning my kids today. I trust You will give me the wisdom I need.

My Finances

God, it seems like every time I try to honor You with our finances, something breaks or an unexpected bill pops up. But Lord, I am bringing our finances under Your covering, and we will continue to honor You because Your Word says, "Honor the LORD with your possessions and with the first produce of your entire harvest; then your barns will be completely filled, and your vats will overflow with new wine" (Prov. 3:9–10).

See over our finances God; we trust You.

The most important thing that happens when we pray a See-Over prayer is we remind our souls God is in control. And I believe, as we pray these prayers, they will help us be more open to the movement of God in our lives.

Note from Nicki: If you visit my blog (www.nicki koziarz.com), under the "freebie" section, I've got an expanded version of these See-Over Prayers in a PDF you can easily download.

The Quiet Quitter

Do you remember in chapter 3 when we looked at what it's like to be a Quitzilla—furious, fed up, and fast to walk away? As we work through the final stages of our third habit, she stays open to the movement of God, there's another quitter we need to identify: the quiet quitter.

The quiet quitter doesn't do the dramatic stomping out of the room, slamming doors, while shouting promises of no returns. It's this quiet place where she starts to step back and draw lines of division in her heart. She slowly cuts herself out of projects, plans, and people. I believe uncertainty with God is the area the quiet quitter eases right into her beautiful new home in Quitville.

This process of learning to stay open to what God is doing can bring out some yucky places in us. But this goes back to our first habit: she accepts the assignment of refinement. There's going to be some things we need refined in order to experience the movement of God in our lives.

I found myself becoming a quiet quitter in my early stages of stepping out in faith with God. I wanted God to use me in big ways; but because of my past, there were a lot of hurt feelings, especially in the church. I constantly felt like leadership was overlooking me because I was "that girl." The one who got pregnant before she was married. While that season of my life was rough for many different reasons, I had some major insecurity I needed to work through. I became a quiet quitter by closing myself off from the church and relationships. I wasn't open to much of anything, let alone God.

But a few years after I got pregnant, I started to have this desire to teach the Word of God. I would start to move forward and attend a Bible study or offer to help out with a project for the women's ministry. Discouragement would show it's ugly head when someone would make a comment about how I was doing things, and I would retreat to the corner, quietly drawing a line in my heart. *I'm not good enough for them.* I would then close my fists at God. *I'll never be good enough for Him.* Does this cycle resonate with you?

Quiet quitters seem to have this large target on their back titled Discouragement. And if they can't find the strength to push through the constant arrows of attack, they will quit forever. A quiet quitter is one who is least likely to stay open to the movement of God in her life.

Lysa TerKeurst, the president of Proverbs 31 Ministries, described this best by saying: "Our character has to match our calling."[2]

The movement is there, friend. God has special assignments that have been put to the side that are just for you. There are things He has placed only you on this earth to do. You are "called." All those years I stayed a quiet quitter, I knew these things, and maybe you know them too.

But is our character ready? This is something every quiet quitter has to discern. Here are some signs quiet quitters may still need to work through their character a little more to match the calling God has for them.

Sign 1: Excuses become their attire of the day.

They start thinking of them the night before, carefully crafting the perfect-way-out explanation. Excuses are their detour around the movement of God. Left unexposed, excuses will one day become the covers for the bed of regret they find themselves lying in.

Sign 2: They stop responding to e-mails, phone calls, and text messages about their commitments.

The commitment starts to feel like it's just not worth their time anymore. They've already quit in their heart so they wonder why they should bother communicating about it anymore.

Sign 3: Attendance at meetings surrounding their commitment becomes less frequent.

When they do come to a meeting, they probably sit in the back of the room, especially away from anyone who might bring out the Quitzilla in them.

Sign 4: They pull back from being around other people who ask too many questions.

The last thing they want is one more person to ask how "that" is going. So if they know or even think you're going to ask about it, they will avoid you at all costs. They may even abandon their grocery cart if they see you at the store. (Not that I have *ever* done such a thing.)

Quiet quitters are closed, closed, closed. Closed to the process, closed to conversations, and ultimately closed to what God is doing.

While I'm most definitely still "in process" of lining up my character to match my calling, there's a verse that has helped me so much. It's Psalm 55:22:

> Cast your burden on the LORD, and He will sustain
> you; He will never allow the righteous to be shaken.

Please don't underestimate the power of this word *sustain*. It's a word we can pray for strength of continued mercy from God on whatever we are trying to accomplish. Just by asking God to sustain us releases mercy, which is a fresh supply of strength.

> Mercy is a fresh supply of strength.

Quiet quitters have a genuine spirit of meekness and often put others before themselves. But often their excuses are concealed as godliness. They are afraid to fight for what's right because of the fear that it will be taken the wrong way. Big personalities intimidate them, and hard situations just make them want to crawl up in a corner.

But when a quiet quitter whispers a See-Over Prayer of, "God, see over me to sustain me," something happens. The urge to quit begins to flee, and all of a sudden something changes.

It's Not Too Late

When I think of all the excuses quiet quitters battle, the excuse of "it's too late" might be their greatest. In those moments a quiet quitter can't see what God is doing, she has the potential to miss what God wants to do through an "it's almost over moment."

I'm not a huge football fan, but when I was growing up, my dad was a high school football coach. So I was doing the *Friday Night Lights* thing since before I could talk. I have a lot of good memories about those football games. One of the things I remember most was, just when we thought the game was over, it wasn't. Someone would call a time-out, go into overtime, and score the winning, unforeseen touchdown. I learned early on that the game always has the potential to *suddenly* shift gears. And ultimately these overtimes brought an unexpected victory to someone.

God is the best with the *"expect the unexpected"* rulings.

If we will learn to stay open to His movement through these hard assignments, He will do something inconceivable in and through them.

It's what we can call an Ephesians 3:20 moment:

> Learning to stay open to God's movement brings powerful, inconceivable moments to our lives.

Now to him who is able to do immeasurably more than all we ask or imagine, according to his power that is at work within us. (NIV)

A quiet quitter has the advantage over a Quitzilla because she will take the time to internally process things before reacting. She has the disadvantage because the process is often overthought and seen as being finished when it's not. But if the quiet quitter can switch her quiet heart from quitting to trusting, everything has the potential to change. *Suddenly.*

Complacent hearts can **suddenly** become revived.

Broken relationships can **suddenly** become restored.

Forgotten dreams can **suddenly** become renewed.

When the quiet quitter starts to rise up in you, remember this: nothing and no one can threaten your purpose in God. The game's not over; it's just running into a little overtime.

> Your game isn't over; it's just running into a little overtime.

Suddenly Naomi

There's a hint of a See-Over Prayer from Naomi in our story. And it comes completely unexpectedly and suddenly. Something is starting to shift in her. Perhaps for the first time in a long time, she's starting to be open to the movement of God in her life.

After a long day out in the wheat field, Ruth comes home filled with excitement. Naomi wants all the details, and so she listens carefully as Ruth fills her in. And then Naomi offers these gentle words:

> "May he be blessed by the LORD, who has not forsaken his kindness to the living or the dead." (Ruth 2:20)

"Who has not forsaken . . ." Is it possible Naomi is opening up her hands again? Is she coming back under the covering to be seen over by God? Are these fists of hers that were so closed to God starting to open up?

I don't know about you, but I'm so excited to see this happening! Naomi, this woman who has displayed all the tendencies of a quitter, is changing.

Fists Open

I have this horrible habit of falling asleep with my fists clenched and my thumbs tucked under my fingers. I don't know if it's something I did as a child or what, but it's like a comfort thing.

Often I'll wake up, and my hands will be sore because I have squeezed them so tightly while sleeping. I've been trying to stop doing this because I read that you can develop arthritis in your hands if you don't break the habit.

When I lay my head on my pillow at night, sometimes I stop and remind my brain, "Fists open." Most of the time if I do this right before I fall asleep, I don't wake up with sore hands. But since this is a bad habit, I often naturally just fall asleep like this.

This process of living under the covering of God is going to require some brain reminders. Staying open to what He's doing is not something that is going to naturally come, especially when things get hard.

Just like it almost feels natural for me to fall asleep with closed fists, it will feel natural to want to control our circumstances around us. Disappointments will make it easier for us to close our fists to God.

A woman whose fists are closed toward the presence of God will often miss:

- The opportunity for God to bless her.
- The chance for God to use her.
- The ability of God to expand her faith and trust in Him.

How open are your hands right now? Maybe you're not ready to completely open your hands, but can you start with something small? Remember, at the beginning of this story, Naomi arrived in Bethlehem with her fists completely closed to God. Slowly she has started to open her hands again. And He's there to meet her, even if it's just her pinky that's come unclenched.

God doesn't meet us at perfection. He meets us where we are in our process toward receiving His promises.

> God meets us wherever we are in the process to His promises.

As we wrap up this chapter and this habit, here are two things I want you to remember about the third habit:

Habit Three: She creates space for the movement of God in her life.

1. Stay open and go low. Surrender and humility are the peanut butter and jelly of our faith. This is a process with you and God, the secret places He's taking you through. Even if it feels like no one is with you through this process, He sees every effort you make. And just like Ruth with Boaz, if someone needs to see it, God will show her your efforts.

2. Come under to be seen over. God invites you to come under His covering so He can see over your life. Trusting God with the outcomes of life doesn't always feel natural for us. But like Ruth, if we remain under the covering of God, He will provide for everything we need.

━━━━━ **Make It Stick** ━━━━━

Living under the covering of God means that we are asking God to "see over" our lives.

See-Over Prayers contain two things: my problem and God's promise.

Learning to stay open to God's movement brings powerful, inconceivable moments to our lives.

━━━━━ **To Be Honest** ━━━━━

Write your See-Over Prayer below:

_____

_____

_____

_____

✓ **Habit One:** She accepts the assignment of refinement.

✓ **Habit Two:** She follows through with her commitments despite how she feels.

✓ **Habit Three:** She stays open to the movement of God.

Habit Four:

Habit Five:

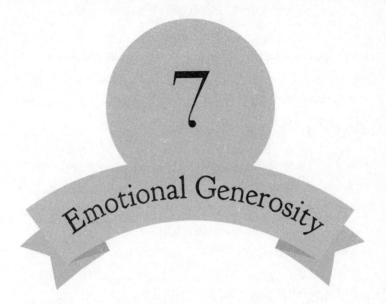

7

Emotional Generosity

Habit Four: She gives others what she needs.

We were out of milk, so I headed to the store with my party of five.

Even though we were in a time crunch, I wanted to make the most of our trip and pick up a few other things. Our family divided up—my husband went to the row of toilet paper, our oldest daughter walked off to get bread, our middle daughter headed out for fruit, and the youngest one, Kennedy Grace, trekked to the milk fridge with me.

Everyone quickly got what they needed and met back at the register—except my husband. At the self-checkout with my three girls, I scanned our items thinking Kris would arrive any second. But he wasn't. As the line behind me quickly grew long and impatient, I wondered if I should cancel my order and step out of line.

Time was short and we were already running late. In this unnerving moment, I instructed my youngest daughter to run and get the toilet paper from her daddy. She took off, found my husband, and secured the rolls under her arm. But on her way back to the self-checkout, a sparkly cereal display distracted her.

In a calm, yet firm voice, I made sure my daughter heard me. "Kennedy Grace, come here right now please."

In her little head she figured the fastest way to get that toilet paper to me was to slide it down the aisle. Without hesitation she whooshed the package right to me.

The people standing behind me thought my daughter's idea was quite amusing. Everyone except one woman.

As Kennedy Grace giggled, jumped, and bounced her way to the register, I knew this wasn't the time or place to have a teachable moment, so I just muttered quietly for her to calm down.

That one woman, feeling it *was* a good time to teach my daughter a lesson, said to me, "Well, isn't she something?"

I didn't want to get into a hot, confrontational mess, so I ignored her and bagged my items.

But then she asked Kennedy Grace, "Why are you acting up so much?"

Kennedy replied, "I'm sleepy."

And then the woman responded with a statement no stressed-out momma needs to hear, "Well, maybe your mom should put you to bed earlier."

What did she just say? Unh-huh. I gulped and took a deep breath, ready to blurt out something sassy.

But in the midst of this chaos, in the midst of this tension, I felt the presence of God hold me back with this thought, *Give her what you need most.*

Say what, God? I need to give this woman a piece of my mind, is what my soul screamed.

But it was true. I need **a lot** of grace these days. Grace. Grace. Grace.

So I said nothing. I extended grace. I smiled, grabbed Kennedy's hand, and walked out of the grocery store, challenged by the thought of Luke 6:38:

> Give, and it will be given to you; a good measure—
> pressed down, shaken together, and running over—
> will be poured into your lap. For with the measure
> you use, it will be measured back to you.

I make a lot of mistakes. I forget about important things. And I too have judged stressed-out mommas in the grocery store with misbehaving children. But that verse in Luke tells us that when we give to others what we need, something freeing happens: **We receive what we need too.**

Or even better, we remember what's been given to us already, and our cup begins to fill.

Emotional generosity is often one of the hardest forms of kindness to give. And our culture certainly does not teach us to do this well. Sassy comebacks with the hashtag #Boom next to it are often the most viral words spoken.

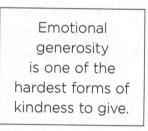

Emotional generosity is one of the hardest forms of kindness to give.

For a woman who struggles with quitting, not being able to give others what we need will paralyze the process toward completion. I like to figure things out quickly. But sometimes because my brain needs an answer, I create an assumption of someone or something, which leads to destruction.

I think the area I struggle with this the most is within my marriage. Kris is a quiet guy. He is fine to only speak about thirty words a day. And if those words are through a text message, even better!

Communication is my number one strength. So I need words. And trust me, I give him plenty. But he doesn't often give them back. So when he's quiet,

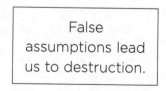

False assumptions lead us to destruction.

I often assume it's because he's mad or I did something wrong. Before I know it, I'm envisioning him quitting our marriage, the packet of divorce papers being delivered to my house, and it makes me all kinds of insecure.

But really what's happening is Kris just doesn't want to talk. Or he's used up his thirty words with his customers or our girls. Pushing Kris with this issue makes him shut down even more, causing more issues in our marriage. I'm learning to give him what he needs, quiet space without judgment. There are times I need this in my life, and he gives it very well.

When we offer emotional generosity to others, we create the atmosphere for God to do something powerful in us and through us. I don't always **want** to give others what I need. My initial reaction is often to give others what I think they deserve: *A quick comeback. A nasty look. An unforgiving heart.*

None of these things have ever brought me anything I needed. All they brought me was more refinement, more hurt, and more issues.

When we feel like others are not giving us what we need, it's really easy to give up. We start to feel resentful and maybe even a little entitled. And so we begin an internal conversation:

If they aren't coming to my dinner party, I'm not going to theirs.

or

If she didn't return my phone call, she better not expect me to return her call.

and

If they are not going to try in this relationship, I'm not either.

Emotional stinginess is easy, and it comes pretty natural to most of us. It starts as kids. Why is sharing such an impossible concept to teach a two-year-old? Like us, they are born with a sin nature pulling them toward themselves: their needs, their desires, their entitlement. As they grow in age and maturity, they'll be able to better understand it.

Emotional generosity is something we will always need to be sowing into our lives. It's something we mature into. It won't be instant. And it may take some time to grow.

She Reaped What She Sowed

I told you at the beginning of this book, the habit I least like in all of this was accepting the assignment of refinement. But I really like implementing and learning more about Habit Four: *she gives others what she needs.*

Giving others what we need is bravery and kindness mixed together. In my opinion it's the greatest form of generosity. It takes some time to get into a rhythm with this habit, but once you do, you'll give everything you ever thought

> When I give others what I need, I'm sowing another life-giving seed.

you needed away. Because you'll see how giving others what you need is sowing seeds of life into this world.

Ruth lived out this habit so well throughout her entire story. And up until this point, she's given a lot of what she's needed to Naomi: kindness, commitment, love, and peace. And now she is about to receive back ten times what she has given.

In the last chapter we saw how Naomi started to open up her hands just a little bit to God after Ruth's great day in the field. I picture Naomi, in a typical motherly tone, inquiring more of Ruth about her day. I also picture Ruth as a babbling schoolgirl, telling Naomi about this hand-some, nice, kind man, Boaz. Okay, the Bible doesn't tell us whether Boaz was handsome, but that's my version of the story, and I'm sticking to it.

Ruth goes on and on about how Boaz invited her to lunch, asked her to keep gleaning in his field, and told her to stick close to his servants for her safety.

Naomi's mouth drops and tells Ruth this is a good thing!

Naomi continued, "The man is a close relative. He is one of our family redeemers." (Ruth 2:20)

A family redeemer was someone who had the privilege, but also the responsibility, to act on behalf of a relative who was in need. So the kindness Boaz showed Ruth to allow her to glean in his field was pretty standard. But the fact that he invited her to lunch and told her to stay with his servants was above standard. There was something special there.

Day after day Ruth finds herself gleaning in Boaz's field, picking up whatever leftovers she could bring home each day. She showed honor and respect to Boaz while staying open to what possibilities might be ahead for her. Naomi is carefully watching this relationship unfold.

Perhaps she is seeing Ruth's longing for the things she needs: security, direction, and a husband. And one day something shifts in Naomi.

> Ruth's mother-in-law Naomi said to her, "My daughter, shouldn't I find security for you, so that you will be taken care of?" (Ruth 3:1)

The unknown author of the book of Ruth leaves Ruth's response to this question a mystery. But directly after this question, Naomi lays out the plan. She's got an idea, and she needs Ruth to trust her.

The Miracle Pig

One of the first things my middle daughter Hope asked for when we moved to the Fixer-Upper Farm was a pig. And one day I got a phone call from a woman who was trying to help find homes for not one but two piggies. They were in an awful situation so there was no way we could say no. We appropriately named them Romeo and Juliet because it was a tragic love story.

There was one small surprise that came with the adoption. Momma pig, Juliet, was expecting. I knew nothing about pigs, pregnant pigs or baby pigs. So the next few months after they came to live with us was filled with more adventure than my first-generation farming heart could handle. We eventually figured it all out, and one day there were four bundles of cuteness oinking around the barnyard.

Princess Jules was the runt of the bunch. And for a few days she seemed to struggle with walking and getting onto her momma's belly to nurse. Squished to the side, trampled by the others, and having to fight hard makes a runt's life difficult.

The day shrieks were coming from the barnyard my heart thumped, and my feet moved quickly. Something about those unheard before squeals set off an alarm in my head. One of those babies was in danger.

Jules was just sitting on the ground unable to move. Her momma, pacing and panicked over the piglet's squeals. I don't know if it was intentional or not, but it had appeared momma pig, Juliet, had stepped on this little runt fairly hard.

I picked up that delicate black-and-white shrieking piglet and wrapped her up in a torn piece of a fleece blanket. Laying her down on the concrete slab, away from the others, I lifted her back legs up and pushed her two front legs to move together. But her strength failed her as she tumbled to the ground over and over.

Things weren't looking too good for her.

My eyes swelled up as I held the phone close to my ear. Young, tender ears were close by, and I knew these words being spoken would crush her heart. The vet presented little hope, only a permanent resolution to her pain.

No, Mommy, no. She held the piglet close as tears fell from her eyes; she offered a song to soothe the piglet's cries:

You are my sunshine, my only sunshine
You make me happy when skies are grey
You never know, dear, how much I love you
Please don't take all my sunshine away.

The same words I had once quietly sung over her troubled soul in the middle of the night. Princess Jules fell fast asleep wrapped in her arms of love and compassion. And we vowed to give Princess Jules the best last days of her life. We bottle-fed her, sang to her, and held her as often as time allowed.

But when a determined little girl prays, it's as if she moves the veil of the throne room back and kneels before the King herself. In our last moment of hope before it was time to call in the vet, my husband had an idea to stop by a nearby neighbor's farm and let him look at the pig.

Farmer Moore did more than give us a piggy checkup. He had raised pigs for many years of his life and had seen a pig momma more than once hurt a baby piglet. So he offered us the perspective that she might have done this because she didn't have enough milk for her babies.

He looked her over a few times and assured us there was no need to call in the vet. He gave us some specific instructions on what to do with her and assured us she would be just fine in a few weeks. Kris had an idea, and Farmer Moore gave us what we needed, direction and hope.

And wouldn't you know it? She was just fine.

Princess Jules is still waddling and oinking her way around the Fixer-Upper Farm today. She still has her princess shrieks, but she's a happy, chubby little thing. And each time I look at her, I'm reminded of how sometimes it just takes **one idea** to move us forward.

As we continue to unpack this fourth habit of giving others what we need, we might need a few ideas. Ideas that will help bring a little bit of hope, determination, and guidance to get us going in the right direction.

I know it's hard to think about giving something you need away. There are aches, longings, and desires you need to see fulfilled in your life. But this habit is key for a woman who is learning to make decisions that lead her toward commitment.

Naomi's Idea

Naomi desperately wants Ruth to have the most important thing she needed: security. Boaz seems like the perfect answer to this need so Naomi has this idea on how Ruth can share her feelings with Boaz.

It was the harvest season, which meant long days and nights for Boaz. And Naomi gives Ruth these specific instructions:

> Wash, put on perfumed oil, and wear your best clothes. Go down to the threshing floor, but don't let the man know you are there until he has finished eating and drinking. When he lies down, notice the place where he's lying, go in and uncover his feet, and lie down. Then he will explain to you what you should do. (Ruth 3:3–4)

The threshing floor was a place the harvested wheat was stored. Most likely Boaz would be asleep there because he was watching over his harvest. While there are many different perspectives on the meaning of these verses, Naomi's specific instructions (whether sexual or not) lead Ruth to inquire of Boaz's willingness to take her as his wife.

Had Farmer Moore not stepped into the picture with some specific instructions, I would have given up on Princess Jules. I assumed her life was over. And sometimes when we are about to make a false assumption and jeopardize a relationship or situation, we need clear guidance.

God, through His Word, gives us some specific, clear direction when it comes to emotional generosity:

1. Do not withhold good from others.

When it is in your power, don't withhold good from
the one it belongs to. (Prov. 3:27)

2. Be generous with what we put out to this world.

Remember this: The person who sows sparingly
will also reap sparingly, and the person who sows
generously will also reap generously. (2 Cor. 9:6)

3. Giving always wins.

"In everything I showed you that by working hard
in this manner you must help the weak and remember the words of the Lord Jesus, that He Himself
said, 'It is more blessed to give than to receive.'"
(Acts 20:35 NASB)

Are You Emotionally Generous?

I have an assignment for you. Wait! Please don't skip
over this section. It's going to give you a clear picture on
how well you are able to give others what you need.

Read the question and circle *yes* or *no*.

1. Does seeing other people happy remind you how
   unhappy you are? Yes or No
2. Do you see people who are pursuing the same goals
   as you as competition? Yes or No

3. When you have an idea, do you keep it to yourself?
   Yes or No
4. If someone else is praised for something you do too,
   do you feel resentful? Yes or No
5. Do you feel discontent when others experience the
   same successes in life you have? Yes or No
6. Did you feel unhappy the last time you heard someone got something you wanted? Yes or No
7. Do you find it difficult to give others compliments?
   Yes or No

Now for the results to help you answer the question: "Is
it difficult for me to be emotionally generous?"

Add up your yes's _____

Add up your no's _____

If you find yourself with more yes's than no's, it's okay.
We all have room for growth and are a work in progress.
Generosity is something we all have to learn. And the more
we experience being emotionally generous with others, the
more we will desire it.

Mistake-'Wich

It's the day that almost ruined me.

I've told you stories about a lot of hard days so far in this
book. But this was one of the hardest in regards to giving
someone what I needed.

What I've discovered about hard days is, they don't stop. Yet I'm always trying to convince myself they do. I get through one hard day and think, *That must be it for awhile.* And I'm so surprised when the next day is completely awful too. These days don't come with a warning, a prerequisite (only the cloudy, rainy days should have permission to be bad), or with a limit as to how many things can go wrong in a day.

In a season when it feels like the world is continually dumping on us, we begin to dump on everyone in our lives.

It had been a series of bad days this particular week. A large unexpected bill showed up, my kids were being incredibly sassy, and work was stressful. I was at home working on a project, clicking away on my computer when something completely unexpected popped up in my e-mail in-box. I clicked open the e-mail, and my heart began to race after reading the first line. The tone of this e-mail was harsh, one of finger-pointing and blaming.

I had made a mistake, and she was *clearly* pointing it out, with the person in charge cc'd on the message. I started to think through what my reply was going to be. There were a dozen of things I wanted to say. I was ready to dump on her. But I paused for a moment and realized something. I knew this woman well. She had never spoken to me like this before. And I had a feeling she was going to feel incredibly regretful for saying the things she said in the tone she did.

I had made a mistake, but I knew, on the other side of my mistake, another mistake was being made on her part.

So I let that e-mail sit there for a day. I didn't respond. And I waited. I gave this person what I needed, grace. Sure enough, the next morning another e-mail popped into my in-box with a sincere apology.

I was grateful, but I also was aware of how quickly one mistake can lead to the next. If I had responded back with a snappy e-mail, more tension would have been created, and it would have become a mistake sandwich. *Mistake* with *mistake* on *mistake* with a little side of *mistake*.

What I needed on that day was grace for the mistake I had made. So I gave her some space and grace and received it back ten times full. As I typed out my response back to her, I was filled with grace. I admitted my mistake and did what I needed to do to make it right.

Sometimes I wonder if breaking the cycle of defeat in our lives is as simple as deciding we are not going to stack mistakes anymore. There will always be slip ups, but deciding to look over "this situation" and determine not to stack mistakes is powerful. One I believe God is all about.

> Breaking the cycle of defeat begins when we decide to stop stacking mistakes.

"I will go before you and level the uneven places; I will shatter the bronze doors and cut the iron bars in two." (Isa. 45:2)

I want to be a woman who thrives, not just survives, through life. Life is tough but so are you. When you give others what you need, God will give you what you need. Keep sowing good seeds, invest well. There's a harvest for your life just around the corner. Follow His instructions and you'll get there.

———— Make It Stick ————

When we give to others what we need, something freeing happens: **We receive what we need too**.

Sometimes when we are about to make a false assumption and jeopardize a relationship or situation, we need specific direction.

Breaking the cycle of defeat begins when we decide to stop stacking mistakes.

━━━━ To Be Honest ━━━━

What do you need?

- A financial blessing? *Be a financial blessing.*
- A friendship? *Be a friend.*
- A kind word? *Give kind words.*
- A cheerleader for your project? *Be a cheerleader for someone else's project.*

8

The Other Side of Me

Did you know it's possible to get demoted from Room Mom to Assistant Room Mom?

It is.

It all started at the school open house. My little pig-tailed daughter and I walked into her new teacher's classroom. She greeted us with a warm smile and told us to look around the room and check out all the papers that were on her desk.

I knew what papers were on the desk, so I quickly made my way there.

And there it was . . .

The purple sign-up sheet listing all the volunteer roles for the year. And with a blank line next to the most coveted spot for all the moms at this school.

Room Mom.

Room Mom seemed like a Pinterest dream come true for me. The chance to be at my daughter's school for all her important events and to unleash my DIY skills!

I couldn't believe the space was blank. It was never, ever blank by the time I got to the open house each year. So I quickly wrote my name down and went home to get my party-momma hat on.

This is going to be the best year ever!

And it was . . . for about four weeks.

In the midst of all the Room Mom excitement, several doors of opportunity opened up for me in other areas of my life. I took on a part-time job, began speaking at events, and my afternoons were spent shuffling kids to this activity and then to that activity.

Before I knew it, I was completely overloaded. I was desperately trying to fulfill all my commitments, including Room Mom. However, returning e-mails in a timely manner became hard, and my availability to help cut out crafts became limited.

And after my Fall FAIL party craft (Pinterest lies. Oh, how it lies!), one of the other moms became increasingly frustrated with me.

Soon after, I got an e-mail from my daughter's teacher explaining that she felt like this other mom might have "more time" to fulfill the Room Mom assignments and suggested I assist her.

Well then.

To be honest, the teacher was right. The other mom could do this Room Mom thing in her sleep. She was great at it! And she did have more time to offer than I did.

Still, something inside me ached in knowing people had become so frustrated with me, and I had no idea. Pride had clouded my vision. I couldn't even see how my overloaded schedule was affecting the people around me. I just kept telling myself I was doing my best.

In reality I needed to admit my overload and ask for help.

Now, when I'm sensing my schedule is overwhelmed, I ask myself the best reflective question I've found:

Right now, what is it like to be on the other side of me?

This question helps me pause, pray, and ask the Holy Spirit to show me anything I need to change. It's the question that helps me step into conflict and see the perspective of the person I've offended or frustrated.

After I answer that question honestly, I take notice of the commitments I've made and adjust them to avoid frustrating the people who are depending on me to fulfill my obligations.

Yes, this question leads to a hard-humble place. But it's also a grace-filled place, one we definitely see Ruth experiencing throughout her story.

In the last chapter we saw Naomi taking her eyes off herself. Because she did that, she was able to give Ruth some ideas and specific instructions to help her win the heart of Boaz.

It's Complicated

As we keep moving through this fourth habit—she gives others what she needs, it might feel more complicated before it feels more doable. The older I get, the more I crave simplicity. I want my house to be simply designed; I want all my products and devices to have simple instructions. And I want to live life at a simpler, slower pace. But you and I both know, the older we get, the more complicated life becomes.

Graduating and getting our first jobs, cars, and houses bring all kinds of complicated decision-making processes. When we get married, mixing two families together can create challenges. Throw a few kids in the mix, with schedules and carpools, and it becomes even crazier. Add in some unexpected medical bills or car repairs, and suddenly life can feel like it's spinning out of control! And I've found quitting quickly follows complicated situations.

> Quitting quickly follows complicated situations.

Things are about to get a little complicated for our girl Ruth. She has been in the assignment of refinement for our entire story, but it's getting ready to go to another level.

After Ruth follows all of Naomi's instructions, she finds herself in a conversation with Boaz at the threshing floor. And Boaz says he wants to marry Ruth. But there's this *little* issue.

According to the law, another relative was next in line who had first dibs on Ruth.

Ugh.

Doesn't it always seem like just when things are about to start working out, something or someone slips in and messes it all up? I hate that.

Maybe Ruth had to pause for a moment, remembering Naomi told her Boaz would explain what needed to be done, and then wait even when she didn't understand fully. Here is Boaz, this man who is just trying to follow the law. He's an honorable man who wants to do things the right way. It could have been easy for Ruth to step in and take a seductive, manipulating approach at this point.

But Ruth had accepted this assignment of refinement. She followed through with her commitment despite how she felt. Her steps created space for God's movement. And the girl sowed more good seeds than anyone in this story.

So why now wasn't God stepping in to give her what she needed most? Why did things have to be so complicated?

Where does God seem to be in these eleventh-hour moments?

This is it, guys; this is the place where a lot of people give up! When we feel like we've done all the right things and God isn't making Himself seen or heard. And if we react too quickly in these types of moments, we could miss what God has for us.

Just Hold on a Second

All this time Ruth has been the cheerleader for Naomi. She's committed to her, she's stayed with her, and she's helped her find hope. And now we see a shift.

We are at the climax of this story, the point where we just aren't sure if this is going to work out with Boaz. Ruth comes home after a late night and fills Naomi in on all the details. I'm sure there was a bit of a bummed-out tone with Ruth.

But Naomi is firm with her. We haven't seen her this invested at any other point in the story. It's like all of a sudden something is alive in her again! While Ruth may feel like everything could fall apart, Naomi offers her this perspective:

Naomi said, "My daughter, wait until you find out how things go, for he won't rest unless he resolves this today." (Ruth 3:18)

"Wait."

Waiting is hard. And we do not live in a culture that teaches us to just wait a second. But again, Ruth accepts another assignment of refinement. She could have given up and told Naomi she was through with this process. And maybe Naomi would have let her quit. I don't know.

But every time we accept another assignment of refinement, we move to a place where we are not moving until God does what He needs to do. For the woman who is discovering the power of giving others what she needs, there's a necessity to understand the waiting process.

We don't know how many months, weeks, or even years Ruth sowed these seeds into Naomi. We just know now she's reaping what she has put out there. In the kingdom of God, there is always a seed and harvest time. But the length of time for the process is a mystery.

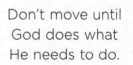

Don't move until God does what He needs to do.

We Don't Wait Well

Do you know how many times a week someone will e-mail me, and if I don't respond in less than thirty minutes, I get a text from them asking if I saw their e-mail?

I can't tell you how many restaurants my husband and I have walked out of because the wait was longer than fifteen minutes. The Internet offers me fast solutions to all my consumer needs. And most of the time, I can have the product by the next day, with free shipping too!

Recently my mom was planning a trip for us, and I was about to loose it with her because she had to have the entire thing planned out eight months in advance. And she wanted every detail planned in less than two days.

I don't plan things out eight days in advance, let alone eight months! I was like, "Can you just hold on a second?!" #loveyoumom

Clearly we do not live in a day and age in which waiting is applauded.

Overall we seem to fear missing out. But I fear we are missing more because we are moving too quickly. We want to see God redeem our lives, but it feels like He's moving at a pace that's too slow for our liking.

So when that person doesn't apologize as quickly as we think she should, we quit giving her our acceptance. Or when we have worked incredibly hard for someone who doesn't take time to say "thank you," we feel justified to start slacking off on the job.

> Overall we seem to fear missing out. I fear we are missing more because we are moving too quickly.

The truth is, we want to see the results of our efforts ASAP. But the return on a lifestyle of emotional generosity is one that is worthy of our patience.

What if Ruth didn't wait? What if she decided she was going to fix this on her own? Boaz, the man who wants to redeem Ruth's life, would not have been able to carry out his plan.

Refinement becomes redemption when we fulfill our responsibility to wait in expectation for the Redeemer to carry out His plan.

Give God your expectations. Wait. Invest. And watch God move.

At daybreak, LORD, You hear my voice; at daybreak I plead my case to You and wait expectantly. (Ps. 5:3)

The Proof

The first person to show me emotional generosity was Mr. Brunn, my fourth-grade teacher.

My family was living in Mannheim, Germany, because my dad had been offered this rock-star teacher position with the military kids. But for whatever reason my parents wanted me to go to a different school. So off the military base, I attended a tiny private Christian school.

I don't have the best memories of this school. I don't know exactly why, other than I seemed to get in a lot of trouble at this school. Especially with my friend Jackie.

We were constantly coming in late from recess, and one time to impress this boy we ripped a Mercedes emblem off a car together. That led to my first and only suspension from school.

But the constant struggle with Mr. Brunn was Jackie and I passing notes in class. We had a pretty good system. Jackie would get up and throw something away and tuck the note next to the pencil sharpener. She'd give me a wink, and then I'd get up to sharpen my pencil.

I'd respond to the note and get up to throw something away, leave the note next to the sharpener, wink at Jackie, and she'd get up to sharpen her pencil.

All was well in our little note-passing world until one afternoon Mr. Brunn caught on to our little method. Mr. Brunn was a German man who looked a little like Santa Claus. He spoke with a deep thick accent and was very kind; he hardly ever raised his voice at us.

But Mr. Brunn had been fussing at me about an assignment. I had to redo the whole thing during recess, and I was so mad because this was going to mess up Jackie's and my cheer routine practice. I was pretty upset with him.

Just as I was about to slip my pink paper under the pencil sharpener, Mr. Brunn looked directly at me. He motioned for me to bring him the note. My heart began to race. Of all the notes for Mr. Brunn to catch me writing, this was the worst one ever. And he had this horrible policy that if he caught us writing notes, he would read them aloud to the class.

I desperately tried to think of an escape route. Could I throw up? Could I faint? There had to be something, anything that would get me out of this tragic mess.

My feet shuffled slowly to the front of the classroom, and with my hands shaking I handed Mr. Brunn the note. He instructed me to sit down while he stood up in front of the class. I put my head down on my desk, and tears filled my eyes.

Mr. Brunn started to read the note, "Jackie, don't you think Mr. Brunn is such . . ." His voice faded off. I didn't think he would finish it but he did! ". . . such an old fart."

He then crumbled the paper with one hand and told me he'd talk to me after class. I was in so.much.trouble. Jackie and I had gotten into way too much mischief that year, and my parents warned me if there was one more incident, there would be a major consequence. And in my head that meant a brutal death.

When the bell for lunch rang, the other kids grabbed their lunch boxes and headed out. I sat at my desk staring out the window imagining what my funeral would be like, who would come, and what they would say.

Mr. Brunn came over and sat down at the desk next to mine. He shook his head at me and ran his fingers through his beard for a moment. I wished he would hurry up and gather his thoughts and release his anger and punishment on me.

But Mr. Brunn said the hardest, kindest words to me in those next few minutes. First, he told me how much those words on that note hurt him. He told me I was better than this and that he saw something inside of me. He knew I needed to stay away from Jackie because she was dragging me down.

I still had to stay inside and redo the assignment. And my punishment for writing the note was I had to stay in from recess the rest of the week.

Mr. Brunn gave me what he needed that day, respect. And something powerful happened in the coming days. I respected that man more than I did anyone in the world. His emotional generosity washed deep over my soul and continues to flow through me today.

Look around you today. There's someone giving you something you need. Like Ruth, you might not be able to see it just yet.

Fight the Right Fight

For several months after I discovered this habit of Ruth, I really worked hard at giving others what I needed. It wasn't always easy, and my flesh tried to convince me this wasn't worth it, but many days I saw the fulfillment of Galatians 6:7:

For whatever a man sows he will also reap.

However, there seemed to be this one relationship where I just never got back what I gave out. I continued to sow and sow and sow. But one day I had it. And I was just about to give up on this relationship for good.

After an intense texting conversation with this person I was ready to give up on, I was driving to an appointment. My phone rang and it was my friend Tina. Tina is one of those friends we don't deserve to have. She's one of the most emotionally generous people I know. I didn't have to tell her anything. She could just tell in that moment there was something I needed, kind words.

And she offered them, more than a dozen. Tina said every word I *needed* to hear. They were words that helped me regain the belief that I could fulfill the assignments God had given me. Words I undeservingly reaped from our relationship.

That day Tina poured into me what I had been pouring out for months. I hung up the phone with her, feeling like a new woman. And it was as if God was giving me a picture of what can happen when we give the world what we need.

Even if emotional generosity doesn't come from the person you desire, God will give it to you from the right person. And it will happen in the most miraculous ways. Remember those "just so happened" moments we talked about before?

It's more of those. And our God has an abundance of them flowing from heaven.

Where you sow your emotional generosity may not be where you reap it. But when a woman who decides to pour into others what she needs, her God is on her side. She is seen, she is heard, she is loved, and she is given what she needs.

When we have what we need, we are able to accept the refinement assignments God gives. When we have what we need, we are strong enough to press through the days that make us want to quit.

I'm afraid our world teaches us to fight for what we want, not what we need. There's a difference. And for women who have the tendency to give in too quickly to the temptation to give up, we have to know how to battle.

Fighting for what we want leads to battles that will leave us completely worn out. They are the internal battles that can lead others and us to forfeit:

- I want to sleep in, but I need to get up and work out.
- I want to drink that Coke, but I need to drink water.
- I want to buy this dress, but I need a pair of socks.
- I want my husband to do nice things for me, but I need his commitment 'til death do us part.

If we don't know what our real needs are in the midst of a battle, defeat will soon follow.

Sometimes it's the simplest things that change our lives the most. And a shift from working toward what we want to working toward what we need has the potential to develop something in us called a *holy ease*.

A holy ease calms the desires to fight in a way that makes us so anxious. It's this place where we begin trusting that God will provide our **needs** and bring the opportunity to experience His faithfulness.

> And my God will supply **all your needs** according to His riches in glory in Christ Jesus. (Phil. 4:19, emphasis added)

See this verse in Philippians is such a good guide to help us remember that chasing our wants will eventually lead us to a place of defeat. But when we ease into trusting God with the results, we will slowly develop the strength to keep going. Through His Word we have what we need to fight the right fight.

In the back of this book there's a list of Quit Quitting verses. Pull those verses out the next time you feel like you don't have what you need, and read those promises over your life.

10 Ways to Be Emotionally Generous

1. Send a text to someone right now telling them something great you love about their life.

2. Allow the person behind you in the grocery line to go ahead of you.

3. At the office put away something your coworker left out.

4. Do one of your kid's chores for them.

5. The next time a friend bails on you, give her so much grace and set her free from worrying you might be upset with her.

6. Write out a prayer for someone who is going through a difficult time.

7. Ask a neighbor before you run errands if there's anything you can do for her.

8. Be responsive in a timely manner with your e-mails/ text messages.

9. Share other people's projects, websites, or ideas on your social media.

10. Before complaining about a problem, think of a solution you could bring to it.

Make It Stick

Quitting tends to quickly follow complicated situations.

Refinement becomes redemption when we fulfill our responsibility to wait in expectation for the Redeemer to carry out His plan.

Where you sow your emotional generosity may not be where you reap it.

To Be Honest

1. Do you feel like you give emotional generosity well?
2. Who is someone who has shown you emotional generosity?
3. What are you waiting for God to redeem in your life?

✓ **Habit One:** She accepts the assignment of refinement.

✓ **Habit Two:** She follows through with her commitments despite how she feels.

✓ **Habit Three:** She stays open to the movement of God.

✓ **Habit Four:** She gives others what she needs.

Habit Five:

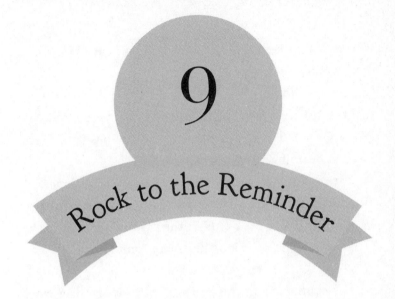

9

Rock to the Reminder

Habit Five: She moves forward in faith.

Midway through our Fixer-Upper Farm-buying process, Mother's Day rolled in. I had been eyeing a pair of rocking chairs at our local hardware store. They were perfect for the Fixer-Upper Farm's front porch. My husband knew how much I loved them, and he had hinted about buying them for me as a Mother's Day gift.

But about a week before Mother's Day, it looked like the whole deal was going to fall through. So I told my husband not to buy me the chairs because it would hurt too much if he did and the deal didn't work out. So I gave him a few other options.

But on Mother's Day morning, I came downstairs to find two black rocking chairs sitting in our living room. My girls were giddy with excitement, and my husband's face was just beaming.

I tried to act so excited. But my heart ached because I didn't want to fall in love with those rocking chairs. Because *what if this didn't work out?* In the card my husband gave me, he wrote the words to our dream coming to life:

It will be as it's supposed to be.

His confidence in this process was way stronger than mine. In my heart I quit our dream more than once. I was ready to give up after round three of closing denial.

But he bought those rockers in faith. And one day we were able to put them on the front porch. Now, when I'm not too sure if God's going to come through, I sit in those chairs. I rock to the reminder that if God did it before, He will do it again. His faithfulness never runs dry.

Even when it looks like the business is about to crumble and the power is about to be shut off. Remember He's a *then God*. He's in the business of stepping in and making things come together.

What God ordains, He sustains.

Sometimes we just have to take some steps in faith.

For we walk by faith, not by sight. (2 Cor. 5:7 ESV)

Hang Tight, Ruth

The fifth and final habit of the woman who doesn't quit is: *She moves forward in faith.* This sounds cliché, I know. But really there is no other phrase to describe what we are about to see lived out at the end of Ruth's story.

Moving forward in faith was the root of her entire story. Ruth's first step of doing something "in faith" was following Naomi to Bethlehem. Then it was the "in faith" step of getting to work without the promise of much.

Her faith has led her to this amazing encounter with Boaz.

Now "in faith" she is going to have to trust Naomi's word of guidance to wait. And in faith she will have to trust that Boaz is going to get this redeemer thing straightened out.

Can you imagine the anguish she must have felt in her soul? The uncertainty she had felt all this time since loosing her husband must have created a sense of urgency to know how this situation was going to turn out. She had two options: quit or hang tight in faith.

Ruth isn't the only person in the Bible who had to learn to move forward in faith. And I love how Hebrews 11 lays out the deep historical roots of those who have gone before us by faith. These are a few of my favorite "by faith" examples.

Hebrews 11:4

By faith Abel offered to God a better sacrifice than Cain did. By faith he was approved as a righteous man, because God approved his gifts, and even though he is dead, he still speaks through his faith.

Hebrews 11:7

By faith Noah, after he was warned about what was not yet seen and motivated by godly fear, built an ark to deliver his family. *By faith* he condemned the world and became an heir of the righteousness that comes by faith.

Hebrews 11:11

By faith even Sarah herself, when she was unable to have children, received power to conceive offspring, even though she was past the age, since she considered that the One who had promised was faithful.

Hebrews 11 has more than a dozen "by faith" examples. And just as Naomi said "in faith" that Boaz would go that very day to meet with this fellow kinsmen redeemer, he did.

Boaz went to the gate of the town and sat down there. Soon the family redeemer Boaz had spoken about came by. Boaz called him by name and said, "Come over here and sit down." So he went over and sat down. (Ruth 4:1)

Maybe you don't need to buy rocking chairs, but is there something tangible you could do to move forward in faith? Whatever it is could be the exact step you need to take in order to help you not quit. Find what makes you rock to your reminder.

I'm Just Tired

The sun was beating down, and we'd been sitting poolside for hours. Two of my daughters, HopeAnn and Kennedy had joined a summer swim league. This was HopeAnn's fourth season, but it was Kennedy's first. Her inexperience was both a good and a bad thing.

Her inexperience with this sport taught her she can push herself a lot harder than she ever imagined. But her innocence also let her believe she could quit if she got tired.

The time for Kennedy's event came. She climbed up onto the diving block, got into her position, and when the whistle blew, she dove into the water. This was going to be the longest event she'd ever swam, and I was nervous for her.

The first lap came, and she swam with all her might to the end of the pool. The second lap came; she swam with all her might to the other end of the pool. The third lap began; she swam with all her might to the opposite end of the pool. But then she stopped.

She stood up in the water and grabbed her chest, as though she were having trouble breathing. My momma heart sank, and I ran over to her side. The coach looked at her for confirmation that she was okay. With her pink goggles pulled on top of her head, she glanced all around the pool and saw everyone else who had been swimming the event finished. And with tears in her eyes, she looked at me and said, "I'm just tired."

Her coach smiled and looked at me. Relief fell on our faces. She was okay. She was just tired. She climbed out of the water and left the event unfinished. Her lawn chair and warm towel awaited her to the side. With the towel wrapped around her, she sat down in the chair with defeat washed on her face.

Tired. She was just tired. I explained to her daddy, the man who runs marathons and never seems to run out of endurance. Sometimes I smile when I think how God who would give this man who pushes through extreme physical limitations four fragile women. So he doesn't get a girl who quits because she's tired.

But I do get it. And I'm willing to admit I believe this is the number one reason why I quit things. *I just get tired.*

Recognize, Rule Out, and Renew

I see three types of tired in women who want to give up.

1. Physically Tired

When we are struggling with physical exhaustion, the first thing we think of when we wake up is: *when can I go back to sleep?* There are all kinds of reasons we could be physically exhausted, but when our bodies are shouting for a slower pace or more sleep, we need to listen.

2. Emotionally Tired

The emotionally tired start to get snappy at things we don't normally care about. We become lethargic and feel like we are just going through the motions of life.

3. Spiritually Tired

Of all the kinds of tired's, this is the one most threatening to a woman who might quit. You feel this kind of tired when your time with God has simply become a routine: go to church, pray, read a Bible verse.

As I've taken the time to look back on my quitting journey, I realized how much being tired has effected my illogical decisions to quit things.

In order to move forward in faith when I'm tired, I have to determine what type of tired I am. After that I can rule out the reasons I'm tired and then take the steps to renew my faith. Below are three steps you can take when you are having a hard time determining the cause of tired.

Step 1. Rule Out the Reasons. I don't mean googling your body symptoms and letting WebMD diagnose you.

Not that we would ever do such things (wink). I mean, it's time for a visit with your doctor. Sometimes a serious underlying issue is battling your body.

At my yearly checkup my doctor almost always says the same things to me: eat better, lose weight, get more sleep. I do deal with anemia so this is something I have to keep a check on when I start to get downright physically exhausted. But your doctor can also help you understand your body better. Do you need to drink more water? Do you have a food allergy you didn't even realize? Are you depressed? These are all the things your doctor can help you understand.

And I know, as the expert quitter, your health is often the least of your worries. You can just pop an Advil, drink another cup of coffee or Coke Zero, and keep going. But eventually the quitting of health will catch up with us.

If your doctor gives you the all clear, move to the next step.

Step 2. Find Rest. Believe me, I know your time is short and the idea of trying to find time to rest feels impossible. But here's what God has shown me about rest: it's incredibly important, and it allows us to produce more. I constantly fight the artificial reality that to do more is to be more. And if I'm

> God rested from completion, not exhaustion.

not careful, eventually exhaustion becomes the banner over my life.

Yesterday I took the entire afternoon off. I spent time outside getting some Vitamin D therapy, holding my family close, and pretty much letting my house stay a wreck. And this morning I woke up with this chapter burning inside of me. I knew God had honored the time I had spent unplugging from the world and to just be present.

Maybe your rest starts with just a few hours, one day a week. Perhaps it looks like turning off your phone, reading a book that fills your soul with good things or being with your friends and family.

What are the things that refuel you? These are the things you need to do when you seek rest. Rest can be more than taking a nap.

I hope that one of the things you feel like refuels you is being part of corporate worship, whether it's a Wednesday night, Saturday, or Sunday service. I know we live in a world that offers online church attendance, and this is great! I've had many Sundays at home, on my couch, with a computer screen and a Bible. And God has been there, and His presence is sweet.

But there is something incredibly valuable about coming together with other people who love God and joining your souls in worship and the teaching of God's Word.

If your church drains you, it might be time to move on or reevaluate all you are doing within the church. I'm not telling you to quit church or your volunteer roles. I'm suggesting you find a rhythm with the church that allows your soul to be rested and renewed by your being part of the church.

After you've taken this step and you still don't feel like you can move forward in faith, try step 3.

Step 3. Take a Day for You. Pulling away from others to pull closer to God is not just something that is beneficial for you; it's something Jesus did:

> Yet He often withdrew to deserted places and prayed. (Luke 5:16)

Often. I wonder how many times? Was it once a day? Once a week? Just when He started to feel exhausted? We don't know, but we know He did this, and the Bible tells us it was often.

A lot of "big thinker" leaders are doing this. They are picking a day, once a quarter, to pull away from social media, work, their families and friends to remember the vision they have for their lives. In their journals they write down where they are right now, where they want to be, and what they need to do to get there.

I've not been able to take a whole day away to do this yet, but I have taken a half day, and it's been so beneficial. I've also started taking an hour or so

> When the demands of life drive us to passionless steps, it's time to pull away.

once a week to sit down and evaluate everything I'm doing. I ask myself some hard questions like: Where am I spending too much of my time? Do the people around me feel loved? What goals am I most focused on right now?

When we get caught up with the demands of life, we want to quit everything because we have forgotten who we are and what drives our passion.

Learning to move forward in faith is going to require some energy and effort on our part. I think there's a misconception that to have faith is to have all the determination in the world. But there is a difference between our effort and His ability. The perseverance of our faith holds the mystery of mercy that to do less is to be more.

> The perseverance of our faith holds the mystery of mercy that to do less is to be more.

Take Another Lap

A few weeks ago I posted a graphic to my ministry Facebook page that caused a stir among people. I've always been vulnerable with the places God is shaping and developing me. One of those places He's refining in me right now is my process of faith. I find myself wanting to skip over the process and just get to the promise that God has for me.

Wouldn't it be nice to just "pull out a promise" every time we needed something from God? But a process comes with each of God's promises. Sometimes the process looks like repentance; sometimes it looks like trust; and sometimes it looks like being unclear about what your next step is.

A phrase that seems to be so big among Christian culture is "faith to move mountains." But I have issues with this phrase because I don't always feel like I have faith that could move mountains. In fact, most of the time I feel like my mountains are not moving. At least not permanently.

- It takes me six weeks to lose five pounds and one week to put them all back on. I have determination, I have plans, but regardless of my faith, with a few bad decisions that mountain will stay put.

- For fifteen years my husband and I have worked on our marriage struggles. But it seems like every time the next fight comes along, more dirt piles on that mountain.

- Let's not even talk about how many times I quit writing this book. Have mercy, you should see my deleted files folder. But throughout this whole process, writing never got easier. No matter how many times I said the name of Jesus. This was hard. The mountain of doubt, fear, and failure at writing did not just disappear.

So on my Facebook page I wrote what God's been saying to me about these mountains not moving:

> Sometimes we want God to move our mountains,
> but sometimes God says, "Take another lap."

We want the mountain to move, but maybe the mountains don't move until the mountain has changed us. The process is change.

But, oh mercy, did this statement cause uproar.

People don't like anyone messing with their churchy statements, and I got all kinds of mad thrown at me. Several *not-so-lovely* messages came rolling in telling me I was misquoting Scripture, and I needed to read my Bible to really understand this promise in Matthew 21:21:

> Jesus answered them, "I assure you: If you have faith and do not doubt, you will not only do what was done to the fig tree, but even if you tell this mountain, 'Be lifted up and thrown into the sea,' it will be done."

I love everything about this verse except the part that says, "If you have faith AND **do not doubt**."

Because here's the part I really struggle with when it comes to my faith: not doubting.

> If our mountains are not miraculously moving, we may need to merge faith with footwork.

Believing God without the tiniest hint of fear, frustration, or uncertainty.

It would be incredibly easy for us to look at all the mountains in our lives, speak to them, and they would simply move. Do my mountains not move because I don't move forward with enough faith? I don't believe so. I think it's because this is one stubborn woman typing these words. And God is still making a lot of changes in my life.

So if your mountains are not miraculously moving either, we may need to merge faith with footwork.

Footwork with faith means we need to never stop taking steps to help our faith grow. For each of us this will look different. Maybe for some it means stepping into a church for the first time or joining a face-to-face Bible study. Others may need to spend more time learning about prayer and worship.

As you move forward in faith, it will feel rocky, shaky, and like it's not making sense. But if you are reading this book right now, then it means I didn't quit. And if you are this far in this book, it means YOU didn't quit.

High fives, friend. One mountain at a time. One lap at a time. No matter how many laps it takes, just keep taking the next step and the next step and the next step.

Stay in Your Lane

The carpool line at my youngest daughter's school is one of the most complicated things I experience during the week. First you must pull into the *S* formation line, then you must pass the J-Crew-Too-Cool-for-School man teacher and watch his hands carefully as he throws you a number. Next you get into the number line he gives you. And if you are the first car in that line, you must line your car precisely up beside the first orange cone. Then you hold up your car tag. Listen for the teacher to call out the next number line for your child to get in. Pass by the obnoxious *move-it-along* waves from teachers, get into the next number line, and voila, you finally have a child climbing into your car.

And it always amuses me when a new car-line parent shows up for pickup. They are just little confused-car-line kernels.

The other day a man in a Honda Pilot was ready to start popping when he realized how complicated the car line was. I just sat there, shaking my head, petting Herman, the slightly famous pug. It was free amusement at its finest.

First the guy pulled into the middle of the two lines, as if he were debating which one to go into. Then he decided to go to the one on the left . . . wait no . . . the right . . . no left . . . no right.

While he was trying to make his directional decision, Mrs. Toyota Siena pulled up behind Mr. Honda Pilot and blew her horn. Then he backed up and finally realized he needed to just pick a line and sit there. Mrs. Toyota Siena rolled her window down in a fury and started to fuss at Mr. Honda Pilot. "You need to pick a lane and just stay there. THIS is how carpool line works. You almost hit my van!"

He shrugged his shoulders at her and put his windows up. Poor guy. He just didn't know what he was doing.

Sometimes I feel like Mr. Honda Pilot. Lost. Confused. Not sure what lane I need to get into. And certainly moving forward in faith will feel this way at times.

I look at the woman in the lane next to me, and her lane looks awesome. She's got a Hummer. So obviously she's cooler than me, minivan mom. And her hair? I think she had one of those fancy Brazilian blowouts, the ones that cost over $100. Her life looks way better than mine; let me get in her lane.

And then I look at the woman in the next lane over. She's got this awesome career. Her Instagram pictures are totally on point. The painting she just created "in her spare time" is phenomenal, and her kids look like they love her so much. Maybe I can scoot on over to her lane.

But there I am in my lane, in my Goldfish-infested van, with dirty hair, and sweatpants I've worn two days in a row. I sit thinking about my laundry piles, the fight I just had with my husband, my whiny kids, the way I'm being treated unfairly by a friend, and I just want to cry. My lane sucks.

There is nothing worse for a woman to do than to compare her life lane with the one next to her. And when we spend time sizing ourselves up to someone else, it will be impossible to move forward in our own faith.

It's those sneaky thoughts that start to pop in. Those thoughts that tell you what you're doing isn't as significant as the person next to you. Or the whisper that in the lane next to you, she already did what you are trying to do. So, why even bother?

My friend, if you listen to no other words in this book, listen to these:

Comparison will always compromise the calling on our lives.

And compromise leads to quitting. I know because I've seen it happen. In my own life and in the lives of others. It's impossible to grow in faith when we lack confidence and trust in a process ultimately producing a confidence rooted in Christ and the race He has for each of us individually.

Say Yes to the Dress

Thank goodness Ruth stayed in her lane. Because Boaz did what he said he would do. He pulled this other kinsmen redeemer to the front of the town and told him all about this situation. And for a moment this relative was ready to take this commitment on.

Until he heard that Ruth was a Moabitess, and this was a package deal. Naomi came with Ruth.

Then Boaz said, "On the day you buy the land from Naomi, you will also acquire Ruth the Moabitess, the wife of the deceased man, to perpetuate the man's name on his property."

The redeemer replied, "I can't redeem it myself, or I will ruin my own inheritance. Take my right of redemption, because I can't redeem it."

At an earlier period in Israel, a man removed his sandal and gave it to the other party in order to make any matter legally binding concerning the right of redemption or the exchange of property. This was the method of legally binding a transaction in Israel.

So the redeemer removed his sandal and said to Boaz, "Buy back the property yourself." (Ruth 4:5–8)

Woo hoo! Ruth girl, it's time to say yes to the dress! The wedding is on. You have won your man. Life is about to be forever changed. And you did it. You saw this commitment all the way through!

━━━━━ Make It Stick ━━━━━

Recognize, rule out, and renew when you're tired.

Sometimes our mountains need another lap.

Comparison will always compromise the calling on our lives.

━━━━━ To Be Honest ━━━━━

1. What is a step you need to take to put some footwork with your faith?
2. What is an area in your life where you are having a hard time not comparing yourself to others?

10

It's Worth It

Almost every summer my husband plans a remarkable Fourth of July party for our friends and family. It's his baby, and he really does enjoy doing it so I stay out of it. Except for all the invite details, food, and such.

He spends hours creating the perfect song/lighting routine to be in sync with fireworks. And he carefully chooses only the best fireworks. You know, the ones that get ooohs and ahhhs from the crowd.

But sometimes planning a party can be incredibly frustrating. You hear of hurt feelings of people who weren't invited, and then about 60 percent of those you do invite don't RSVP or show up. And then there's the potential for rain. It seems like almost every July 4 there is some call for rain!

We spend hours setting things up, preparing food, and then sitting on the edge of our seats wondering if we'll all be crammed under a small pop-up tent for the night. And the clean-up process is a half-day event too.

So each year we evaluate, is this worth it?

Most years we say an astounding YES! But this past year we weren't so sure.

The weather was as close to perfect as it can be for a July summer night. A breeze cooled off the soaring temperatures. The conversations were sweet, the kids were having a blast in the pool, and the patriotic-looking food turned out great. But really we were all on the edge of our seats waiting for the much-anticipated Kris Koziarz firework show.

As the sun began to set and the last drop of light filled the sky, we all grabbed our lawn chairs and blankets and made our way from the backyard to the front yard. It was time to get ready for the fireworks!

But I could tell Kris was a little anxious. He was running around trying to pull all the last-minute details together. And the guy who was going to help him run the show couldn't come so he had asked two other guys to help out.

Kris set the two guys up with a blowtorch to light the fireworks, and he was going to run the lights and music. So together they began the show.

But right away I started to notice something wasn't right with the firework display. Two or three went off, and they seemed to be malfunctioning. As in they were blowing up IN THE GRASS. So I ran over to Kris and asked him what was going on. He thought maybe the guys were putting the fireworks in upside down so he paused his lights and dashed over to help them figure it out.

The show continued, and everyone seemed to be having a great time. In fact, our church campus pastor, Alan, was even scoping the show on Periscope. If you don't have Periscope, it's a live video feed app you can use to stream whatever you are doing. *So awesome.*

After years of having these parties, I felt like we were all sitting way too close to the fireworks. They just seemed to be coming up over us too close. My heart was thumping pretty fast.

I looked over to the side where Kris was, and I could tell he was frustrated. His carefully planned-out music was supposed to be in sync with the lighting of the fireworks. The guys helping him were having a hard time lighting and setting things off to the speed he had set.

I knew he had worked so hard on this show so I just stayed in my seat and didn't bother him with my too-close-for-comfort concerns.

After a few tries, it seemed like the guys helping Kris started to get the hang of it and boom, boom, boom, boom!

The sky over the Fixer-Upper Farm was beautiful, glowing, and so sparkly. Everyone was cheering and all seemed well.

But midway through, one of the fireworks fell over after it was lit and the entire crowd suddenly had a 3–D fireworks experience.

We almost killed our campus pastor, Alan! Who caught it all on Periscope. The firework shot directly at him.

We stopped the show to make sure everyone was OK, which thank goodness they were. Pastor Alan had a chip on his glasses and a little burn on his leg but overall was ok.

Kris assumed it was just a weird malfunction of the fireworks and things would be fine to finish up the show. But my heart, which had almost jumped out of my throat, just really wanted the whole thing to be over.

They continued to light the fireworks, and then . . . it happened again! The firework came straight toward the crowd. This time it exploded completely before it got too close. But everyone was terrified. I ran over to Kris and told him he would either need to shut this show down, or he would need to go over and light those fireworks himself.

He left the lights and music and ran over. But just as he did, the guys had set another firework off, and this time it went straight over toward the cars that were parked on the right side of our farm!

Smoke and flames started to crackle in the grass, and I yelled across the lawn for Kris not to light one more firework while a few of us stomped on the grass to put the flame out!

As my foot was burning from stomping the fire out, this guy yelled out, "Oh, calm down everyone; it's just a little fire." My eyeballs were about to pop out of my head. Are you kidding me? Calm down? A little fire?

This was a disaster.

Immediately a few people packed up their chairs, got in their cars, and left without even saying good-bye to us. My friend had to excuse herself because she had a little mishap with bladder control. Kids were crying, and one little girl let Kris have it. She told him she didn't appreciate him almost blowing her head off!

My stomach felt sick.

I walked around telling everyone how sorry we were. Most of the people were so gracious, understanding, and shared their own firework fail stories.

The teenagers thought this was the most epic party ever. I mean, they almost died at a party, how cool was that?! A few others crowded around the Periscope live feed to replay the fiasco and were laughing until their bellies hurt.

But I just stood there, numb, thankful no one had gotten hurt but so incredibly sad we had upset people. After everyone had cleared out, around midnight, Kris and I sat down in our white Adirondack chairs next to the pool.

I knew I needed to be fragile with the words I said to him as we processed everything that went wrong. He was so disappointed. All the hours of hard work he put into this party had seemed to be ruined.

So I looked at him and said, "But was it worth it?" He sat there for a few minutes, shaking his head, and said, "I don't know."

I don't know.

Will we ever know if it was "worth it" to have that party? I don't know. Were memories created? Oh yes. Did everyone seem to have a good time until the fireworks? Yes. Did we enjoy being with our friends and family? Yes, yes, yes.

But as I think about those people who packed up and just left without even saying good-bye, something in me aches. It was like this picture of someone, without saying a word, assuring you, this was not worth it.

And as I think about you, on the other side of these words, trying to move forward in faith. I feel like you will, at some point, ask yourself, *Is this worth it?*

It's almost a guarantee you will end up at this place as you continue to live out these five habits. All of your hard work will seem to bear no results. Things won't go as you planned. People may pack up and leave your party. Someone you love may sin against you. Standing up for truth may cost you relationships or even your job. Faithfulness to your job may not be enough to prevent you losing your job.

Mess with Your Hopelessness

Is it worth it? Are these commitments we have made to God and others really worth fighting for? Even when it seems like there's no hope, no sign of reconciliation or even progress?

Sometimes I'm not so sure.

But then I read verses like Galatians 6:9, and it just messes with my hopelessness.

So we must not get tired of *doing good*, for we will reap at the proper time if *we don't give up*.

Here's the hard truth: perseverance doesn't always guarantee us desired results. But whenever we have the chance to do **good things**, we should.

While I get tired of inviting people to parties who don't even take a minute to RSVP but get their feelings hurt when they aren't invited, I know community is **good**. I keep putting myself out there to others, even when it's not returned.

I know it's **good** to keep my body heading in the right direction so I fight through the tired of working out, eating right, and seeing few results.

My husband and I are tired of having to work through our differences. We struggle; we fall short almost every day. But we know it's **good** for us to keep trying to work through this commitment. There are things in your life you must keep doing, or even do them more, because we are free and able to do good. Galatians 6:9 points us back to the reward we have as followers of Jesus.

Ruth, the #Wifie

Boaz took Ruth and she became his wife. (Ruth 4:13)

Even though we don't know who the author of Ruth is, I feel like it must have been a man. Because hello, they left out all the good details. Like the wedding!

Oh what a day that must have been for Ruth. To have seen this journey from start to finish. And now here she is ready to begin a new life with this new man. While this long-awaited day must have felt hopeful, I wonder if it was a little bittersweet.

She accepted the assignment of refinement. Her feelings didn't dictate her level of commitment. She stayed open to the movement of God. Ruth gave others what she needed. And she moved forward in faith.

When a woman decides she's going to follow through with a commitment no matter what, her life has the potential to look different. And maybe at this point Ruth feels like all this was worth it. But she has no idea just how worth it this new life will become.

Do You Think You're Worth It?

Do you have goals? Dreams? Hopes? I have a list I keep to revisit and review regularly. It helps me remember the things I want most in order to live out the unique call God has placed on my life. I want you to think about what you want most for your life.

Write down the one thing you want for your life more than anything else right now:

_____

Gosh, this is the part of book writing I don't like. I want to know what you wrote on that line above more than my daughters want to know what presents I've hidden in the closet for gifts! If we ever meet in person, promise me you'll tell me what's on your line.

Do you believe you are worth whatever you desire? Like, really. I'm not talking about a "yeah, I know it." I'm talking about a YES, I believe with all my might I'm worth this.

It's time to take back our lives. Where God restores what has been stolen. The hurt, the lies, the rejection, the disappointments, the failures . . . oh they are still there. But today God is stirring something fresh inside of you.

I think if Ruth or Naomi were to fill out that line above, more than anything they wanted their lives to be redeemed. By God's grace their greatest hope came true.

Boaz took Ruth and she became his wife. When he was intimate with her, the LORD enabled her to conceive, and she gave birth to a son. (Ruth 4:13)

And while Boaz by himself was a great plan of redemption, God wants to do even more.

You Need Therapy Too

My friend Wendy is a therapist. It's a good thing to have a friend who is a therapist because she will often swap therapy for pool dates or dinners.

The other day I was struggling. I was following through with one of my commitments despite how I felt, I was giving others what I needed, and I was embracing this season of refinement. But I was miserable. And I mean m-i-s-e-r-a-b-l-e.

It seemed like no matter how much time I spent with God, filled myself with good thoughts and made good choices, my soul was just in turmoil. My head felt like it was always spinning, my heart was frequently racing from anxiety, and all I wanted to do was quit and sleep.

One afternoon I texted Wendy and asked if I could talk to her for a few minutes. She called me right away, and it wasn't long before tears were dripping down my cheeks.

> Misery multiplies the desire to quit.

First, I asked her not to be my friend for this conversation. I needed someone to look into this from an outside perspective. Then I just started talking. And I didn't like the words that were coming out of my mouth.

I was honest with her about the places I just wanted to quit. It seemed like there were two areas of my life that were constantly making me miserable, and I couldn't figure out how to get through them. You know how some things you quit, and it's not that big of a deal? Well, quitting either of these situations just wasn't an option without major negative consequences.

She asked me some hard questions, and I gave some hard honest answers.

Wendy gave me some great advice that afternoon. But the most important thing she said to me was, "Nicki, sometimes you just need to look back and remember the places God has brought you through."

There's a quote that says, "The greatest teacher in life is your last failure." And so after she said those words to me, I took a moment to think back on the last time I quit, the last time I failed, the last time I gave up. I remembered how I felt when I quit.

Just because you miss something the first time, the second time, or even the third time doesn't mean it's over. While I believe strongly in the power of these five habits, these habits aren't magic.

Just One Percent

I'm all for setting goals and making plans for the lives we want to become a reality. I love vision statements and life maps, but I have also discovered the power of a woman who does just *one thing*.

The other advice my friend Wendy, the therapist, gave me that day was this concept called: the power of 51 percent.

If *success* can be redefined as "not quitting," it's this idea that if we can just stay *1 percent* above 50, we are heading in the right direction.

One percent above the line.

I can do this. You can do this.

Let's break this down.

Today you wake up, and you want to stop quitting your workout program. You're battling the reality of exhaustion, and sitting on Facebook seems like it would be a lot more fulfilling for thirty minutes. But you've also committed to this process of becoming a woman who doesn't quit so you pull out your no-quitting verses (in the back of this book), and you remind yourself that God chooses you. Handpicked for a special purpose. And He's counting on you to become a woman who follows through with Him.

So, while you determine in your spirit you can't handle Jillian Michaels' bossy commands today, you choose the 51 percent route and go for a quiet walk. No, you didn't give everything you had, but you gave it 51 percent, and so that's a step in the right direction.

If today you just can't give it 100 percent, just give it 51 percent.

Quitting is not your story. It's a chapter, it's a blog post, but it's not who you are. I don't care what you've quit; nothing is ever too late for God to turn it around. Nothing.

Your worth is not defined by what you've already quit, how many times it takes you to get this thing completed, or who is moving faster than you.

Moving forward in faith is to just keep doing the next hard thing.

You Can't Even Imagine

You can't imagine the possibilities as you embrace this fifth and final habit of the woman who doesn't quit: *She moves forward in faith.* Ruth could have never imagined either.

First, she falls in love and marries this amazing man, Boaz. But God wasn't finished there. Then she becomes pregnant and has a son, and Naomi's life is transformed from bitter to blessed. But God wasn't finished there either.

> Naomi took the child, placed him on her lap, and took care of him. The neighbor women said, "A son has been born to Naomi," and they named him Obed. He was the father of Jesse, the father of David. (Ruth 4:16–17)

Here is what can happen when one woman sticks with a commitment the entire way:

The Genealogy of David

Now this is the genealogy of Perez: Perez fathered Hezron. Hezron fathered Ram, who fathered Amminadab. Amminadab fathered Nahshon, who fathered Salmon. Salmon fathered Boaz, who fathered Obed. And Obed fathered Jesse, who *fathered David.* (Ruth 4:18–22)

David = the ancestor to *Jesus!*

God brought Jesus, the Savior of the world through THIS **generational** line. Ruth, the woman who didn't quit.

If God could do something so powerful through Ruth, He can do the same through you and me. When we refuse to settle for the blows life offers us, we make the decision to move forward in faith. It's going to be more than we could ever imagine or dream.

But maybe in order to get there, we are going to have to make a decision that now things are different.

She Decided Today Was Different

It's the same stupid fight again and again.
You were supposed to stop by the store; I was supposed to pick this kid up.

It's the redundant load of laundry again and again.
The missing socks, the torn jeans, and the
spaghetti-stained shirt.

It's the predictable drive to and from work again
and again.
Wait for the light to turn green, pause for the train,
make that last phone call of the day.

It's the expected social media feed.
I'm mad at the government, no one likes me, see
where I am and you're not.

Dear life, you can wear a girl's passion down.

That same girl lays her head on her pillow; she drifts off to sleep, dreaming of being in another place, in another season. The moon drifts over her house. And then the sun peeks through her blinds at an early hour.

And this verse is stirred within her:

"Look, I am about to do something new; even now it is coming. Do you not see it? Indeed, I will make a way in the wilderness, rivers in the desert." (Isa. 43:19)

And she decides, today is going to be different.

Sometimes life needs a new rhythm.
Look, I am about to do something new.

Sometimes we need to see what's happening
around us.
Even now it is coming.
Sometimes our defeat has clouded our vision.
Do you not see it?

May we never forget the power of the gospel message. How following Jesus isn't meant to just make us feel better. It's a path of continual renewal.

The world offers us a slew of paths to make our lives more fulfilling. But at the end of each of those paths is the same result: more wilderness, more quitting.

Women who stay with God are not looking for the same path everyone else travels down. We are looking for a new way in the midst of normalness.

It's time for God to do a new thing in us.

We need a path that leads from **faith to faith**.
I will make a way in the wilderness.
On the path we find God in the mundane,
everyday moments of life.
Rivers in the desert.

And our passions for God, others, and following through with our commitments are renewed.

I want to stay on the path of faith to faith. It allows me to find hope in the expectation of the possibility that today, tomorrow, and the next day can be different.

No matter how many times we've quit, no matter what we've already given up, and no matter what we think is over.

Today can be the day of new beginnings.
Today can be the day of renewal.
Today can be the day of an increased presence of God in our lives.
Today can be the day we just decide, trust we'll look back knowing it's when things started being different.

And Now We Go

It's hard to believe we are at the end of this book. But really friends, this is just the beginning for each of us. I've got goals, dreams, and plans to fulfill, and so do you. I believe God has given us everything we need to keep going or to get started.

I'm so proud of you for completing this journey. Look, you didn't quit something. You are different, changed, and a woman who is ready to impact this world in the name of Jesus.

We, these women, who have decided to lock arms and become women God and others can count on. Yes, we will be the ones who impact this world for the good.

We may only exchange glances in the carpool line or at the grocery store or pass by social media posts. But I have a feeling we'll know one another. I'll know by the fruit of your life, and you'll know by the fruit of my life: that's a woman who didn't *quit.*

Until we meet again.

Love,

Nicki

Make It Stick

The perseverance of our faith holds the mystery of mercy that to do less is to be more.

If our mountains are not miraculously moving, we may need to merge faith with footwork.

Comparison will always compromise the calling on our lives.

To Be Honest

1. In what areas of your life do you believe God is asking you to move forward in faith?
2. What is something you can give 51 percent at today?

✓ **Habit One:** She accepts the assignment of refinement.

✓ **Habit Two:** She follows through with her commitments despite how she feels.

✓ **Habit Three:** She stays open to the movement of God.

✓ **Habit Four:** She gives others what she needs.

✓ **Habit Five:** She moves forward in faith.

Quit Quitting Verses

For the time you want to quit because you think too much has already been lost:

> I will repay you for the years that the swarming locust ate, the young locust, the destroying locust, and the devouring locust—My great army that I sent against you. (Joel 2:25)

For the time you want to quit because it looks hopeless:

> So that having been justified by His grace, we may become heirs with the hope of eternal life. (Titus 3:7)

For the time you want to quit because you don't feel smart enough to make the right decision:

> If any of you lacks wisdom, you should ask God, who gives generously to all without finding fault, and it will be given to you. (James 1:5 NIV)

For the time you want to quit because you think you've fallen too far:

> Though a righteous man falls seven times, he will get up, but the wicked will stumble into ruin. (Prov. 24:16)

For the time you want to quit because something else looks better:

> You did not choose Me, but I chose you. I appointed you that you should go out and produce fruit and that your fruit should *remain*, so that whatever you ask the Father in My name, He will give you. (John 15:16)

For the time you want to quit because your efforts and formulas are not turning out as hoped:

> "For My thoughts are not your thoughts, and your ways are not My ways." This is the LORD's declaration." (Isa. 55:8)

For the time you are about to quit because you are going for what you want rather than what you need:

> And my God will supply all your needs according to His riches in glory in Christ Jesus. (Phil. 4:19)

For the time you want to quit because you aren't sure this is worth it:

> So we must not get tired of doing good, for we will reap at the proper time if we don't give up. (Gal. 6:9)

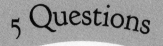

5 Questions

Have I accepted my assignment of refinement?

Am I able to follow through despite how I feel?

But have I stayed open to God's movement?

I don't have what I need, but am I giving what I need?

Truthfully, have I moved forward in faith?

Not quitting is a HABIT!

Notes

Chapter 1

1. According to a new survey commissioned by the American Institute for Cancer Research (AICR), an overwhelming majority of Americans say that the events of September 11, 2001, have not had a significant long-term impact on their day-to-day eating habits, for good or ill. However, one in ten Americans say they gained weight in the months immediately following the attacks, and most are still struggling to lose those extra pounds. See http://www.charitywire.com/charity10.

2. Lysa TerKeurst, *Made to Crave* (Grand Rapids, MI: Zondervan, 2011.

3. Proverbs 31 Online Bible Studies, www.proverbs31.org/online-bible-studies.

Chapter 2

1. Elevation Church, Pastor Steven Furtick, "Don't Stop On Six," www.elevationchurch.org/sermons.

Chapter 3

1. Pharrell Williams, "Happy," 2014.

2. PTED, https://en.wikipedia.org/wiki/Posttraumatic_embitterment_disorder.

3. Mayo Health Clinic article on bitterness, http://www.mayoclinic.org/healthy-lifestyle/adult-health/in-depth/forgiveness/art-20047692.

Chapter 4

1. Definition of *apathy*, see http://dictionary.reference.com /browse/apathy.

2. Typos article: "What's Up With That: Why It's So Hard to Catch Your Own Typos," see http://www.wired.com/2014/08 /wuwt-typos.

3. Tom Rath, *Strengths Finder 2.0* (Gallup Press, 2007).

Chapter 5

1. See Backtoeden.org.

Chapter 6

1. Definition of *atonement cover*, see http://the-tabernacle -place.com/articles/what_is_the_tabernacle/tabernacle_ark _of_the_covenant.

2. Message given by Lysa TerKeurst to her staff at Proverbs 31 Ministries.

Special Thanks

First, to my husband Kris, the man who never quits on me. Thank you for this beautiful, messy, life we live. You are the greatest gift God could ever give a broken-down girl like me. Not a day passes when I don't realize how blessed I am to have you as my husband.

My three beautiful girls Taylor, Hope, and Kennedy, you make me smile more than you will ever know. I'm so proud to call each of you my daughters. You challenge me, you keep me on my knees, and you give me lots of good stories to tell. I love being your Momma K, Madre, Mommy, Mom, and Mother; it's the greatest privilege of my life.

Mom and Dad, thanks for always making me believe I could do anything.

Lysa TerKeurst, my heart will always overflow with gratitude for the day you put your gentle hand on my fragile, rejected-writer shoulder. This book truly would not have been possible without you. Your kindness and support for this project mean more to me than you will ever know. I only hope one day I can bless someone else in the way you have blessed me. Thank you.

Karen Ehman, Holly M., Shelly F., Wendy P., Kristi D., Wendy G., Tina, Renee S., Lynn C.: Your texts, e-mails, and real-life encouragement have flowed into these rivers of words. Any woman who has you as a friend is blessed.

To Nicki's No-Quit Girls, thank you for all your honesty and your responses to my 911 book-question e-mails. You were such an encouraging and fun part of this writing process!

Sheila Magnum, that day, the pinky promise? I love you to the moon and back.

Amy Lykins, your wisdom and honesty for this project were priceless.

Lisa Whittle, thank you for being the first person, other than my mom (smile), to believe in me as a writer. Just a few words: boxing gloves, bat, and flan.

Lisa Allen, your encouragement and support go beyond a word of thanks. Your gift of leadership is one I'll always hold close. Thank you for your constant support, love, and encouragement through this process.

Melissa Taylor, I could have never imagined how a tearful conversation in a closet would literally turn into an office of dreams. You've been there with me every step of the way, and I'm forever grateful to you for taking a chance on this girl who just had a lot of ideas.

Angie, Laurie, Steph, and the entire Proverbs 31 Online Bible Studies team, thank you for letting me be part of such an amazing movement of God! It's absolutely an honor to serve alongside you crazy, God-loving women.

To the speaker, writer team, and staff at Proverbs 31 Ministries, you are the best team to serve shoulder to shoulder with. I love each of you, and I'm honored to call you teammate.

And last but not least, thank you B&H and LifeWay for taking a chance on this girl who just had a dream to share words.

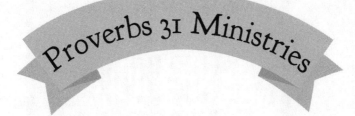

Proverbs 31 Ministries

If you were inspired by *5 Habits of a Woman Who Doesn't Quit* and desire to deepen your own personal relationship with Jesus Christ, I encourage you to connect with Proverbs 31 Ministries.

Proverbs 31 Ministries exists to be a trusted friend who will take you by the hand and walk by your side, leading you one step closer to the heart of God through:

- Free online daily devotions
- First 5 app
- Daily radio program
- Books and resources
- Online Bible Studies
- COMPEL Writers Training: www.CompelTraining.com

To learn more about Proverbs 31 Ministries call 877-731-4663 or visit www.Proverbs31.org.

Proverbs 31 Ministries
630 Team Rd., Suite 100
Matthews, NC 28105
www.Proverbs31.org

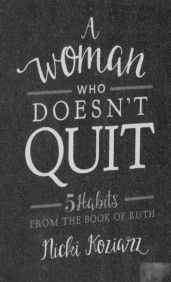